THE ROUNDER BOOK OF BLUEGRASS MUSIC TRIVIA

By Bill Nowlin

The Rounder Book of Bluegrass Music Trivia

By Bill Nowlin

Copyright 2016 by Bill Nowlin

Cover and book design by Gilly Rosenthol

Photography by Bill Nowlin, except as noted.

Cover photograph taken at Thomas Point Bluegrass Festival, September 2013.

ISBN 978-1-57940-251-8
(Ebook ISBN 978-1-57940-252-5)

Bluegrass music
Rounder
First edition

ROUNDER BOOKS

Rounder Books
29 Lancaster Street
Cambridge, Massachusetts 02140
Printed in the United States of America

DEDICATION

To Ken Irwin and Marian Leighton Levy, fellow Rounders
and co-founders of Rounder Records

INTRODUCTION

I came up with the idea for a book of bluegrass trivia back in around 2012. A publisher had approached me back in August 2009 about doing a Boston Red Sox baseball trivia book. Black Mesa Books published it that October, just two months later, and it's done surprisingly well over the years. The book is entitled *Boston Red Sox IQ: The Ultimate Test of True Fandom* and, like this one, it's available in Print on Demand format and via e-books. In fact, it did so well they asked for a second volume, which was published in February 2011: *Boston Red Sox IQ: The Ultimate Test of True Fandom (Volume II, Curse in the Rearview Mirror)*, also by Black Mesa.

They were fun to write and rather soon thereafter, I thought to myself, "Hey, what about a book of bluegrass music trivia?" This is the result. Along the way, I started writing it as the "Bits and Pieces" column in the venerable *Bluegrass Unlimited* magazine, beginning with the issue of July 2013, and the monthly feature has been running for 2 ½ years now. Sometime, I'm sure, I'll run out of questions, but this book contains over 250 of them, as you can see.

It's been fun getting the occasional suggestion, and encouragement, along the way from people like Ron Thomason and Dick Spottswood. Suggestions for future *Bluegrass Unlimited* "Bits and Pieces" are more than welcome — there's no monopoly on good ideas. Send me your ideas. If I use one, I'll want to be sure to give you credit.

Meanwhile, enjoy these! There would be a special prize for the reader who gets the most correct. But I've got no interest in setting up a system to try and monitor that. So, just have fun, and good luck.

A WORD ABOUT ROUNDER

You may ask: What is this word "Rounder" in the title of the book? OK, probably you didn't ask. But in case you have been in hibernation for quite some time, it's named after Rounder Records, the record company founded by Ken, Marian, and myself (see the dedication) in 1970. We recently celebrated our 45th anniversary in October 2015, but without even a 45-rpm record released on the date.

I'd list all the bluegrass albums released by Rounder over those 45 years (and counting), but the list would have more than twice as many items on it as there are trivia questions in this book. None of us can count that high, but Rounder has released over 500 bluegrass and old-time country albums in our time, part of a body of well over 3,000-4,000 record albums. If you figure we released only 500 albums, and the average bluegrass album has maybe 12 tracks, then that's more than 6,000 bluegrass songs or tunes. If you figure the average track lasts 3 minutes and 18 seconds (I just made that up), that's 1,188,000 seconds of music. And if a Lester Flatt G-run takes maybe a second to render, and it takes a little under two seconds for a "shave and a haircut," and if there are maybe an average of five musicians performing during each of those seconds, it could be 10,000,000 or more individual musical notes played.

I have the sense I'm going astray here. Suffice it to say, Rounder put out a lot of bluegrass music. We hope you have some, and that you enjoyed it. Not all the music referred to in these questions is from Rounder. Not at all. But a healthy percentage of it is. And you are most welcome to sample Rounder's wares by visiting any superior record store, or the various online sources. You are invited to www.rounder.com to see currently available bluegrass, and other musics, from Rounder and explore the catalog as well as be on the mailing list for news about new recordings.

Thanks for assistance with the graphics to Linda Shaw and *Bluegrass Unlimited*, and to Jimmy Hole, Eliza Levy, and Matt Miller of Rounder.

FEEDBACK

I welcome feedback about this book, including ideas for other questions, arguments about questions and answers. Write me at bnowlin@rounder.com

—Bill Nowlin

QUESTION 1

How many strings are there in the prototypical five-piece bluegrass band?

QUESTION 2

True or false: the first multi-day bluegrass festival was held on a horse farm in Virginia in 1965.

QUESTION 3

Who was the promoter of the first multi-day bluegrass festival?

    A.   Pete Kuykendall
    B.   Carlton Haney
    C.   Dick Freeland
    D.   John Delgatto
    E.   Jim Clark

QUESTION 4

Can you name the members of J.D. Crowe and the New South at the time of their groundbreaking first album on Rounder?

- A. J.D., Ricky Skaggs, Tony Rice, Doyle Lawson
- B. J.D., Bobby Slone, Mike Bub, Tony Rice, Keith Whitley
- C. J.D., Keith Whitley, Ricky Skaggs, Tony Rice, Bobby Slone
- D. J.D., Jerry Douglas, Tony Rice, Bobby Slone, Jimmy Gaudreau
- E. J.D., Tony Rice, Bobby Slone, Ricky Skaggs

One thing seems certain from the first choices:
Tony Rice was in the group.

QUESTION 5

What year did *Bluegrass Unlimited* begin publication?

    A. 1966

    B. 1970

    C. 1945

    D. 1959

    E. 1969

QUESTION 6

Who was the first bluegrass artist depicted on the cover of *Bluegrass Unlimited*?

    A. Bill Clifton

    B. Bill Monroe

    C. Red Rector

    D. The Sauceman Brothers

    E. Carter Stanley

QUESTION 7

What was Dave Freeman's day job during the first years of County Records?

F.   Instrument repair for George Gruhn in Nashville

G.   Sorting mail on overnight runs between New York City and Pittsburgh for the Railway Post Office

H.   Mandolin player for the Smokey Valley Boys

I.   Radio disc jockey for WWNC and the Wheeling Jamboree over WWVA

J.   Worked at various positions for Rebel Records before starting his own label

QUESTION 8

What was the first Japanese bluegrass band to establish itself in the United States?

A.   Run Mountain

B.   Akira Otsuka

C.   B.O.M. Service

D.   Bluegrass 45

E.   Moonshiner

F.   Fuji Mountain Breakdown

QUESTION 9

Who was Bill Grant's singing partner?

    A.   Wilma Lee Cooper

    B.   Bill Harrell

    C.   Eddie Adcock

    D.   Raymond McLain

    E.   Delia Bell

QUESTION 10

Who is the alter ego of Gordo Noneaux?

    A.   Pete Wernick

    B.   Ron Thomason

    C.   Curtis Burch

    D.   Ray Goins

    E.   Fred Bartenstein

QUESTION 11

True or false: Every single one of these musicians once played in Buzz Busby's band: Eddie Adcock, Jack Clement, Bill Emerson, Pete (Roberts) Kuykendall, Leon Morris, Pete Pike, Scotty Stoneman, and Charlie Waller.

QUESTION 12

How many strings are there on the 5-string banjo?

- A. Five
- B. Four
- C. Six
- D. Eight
- E. None

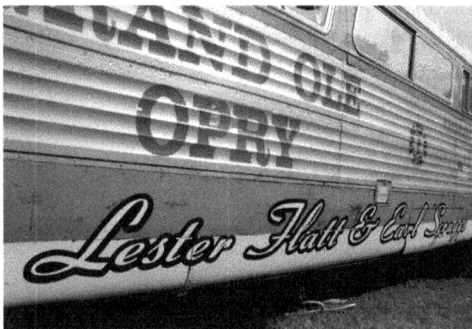

QUESTION 13

Which one of the following was not a member of the New Grass Revival?

A. Sam Bush
B. Ebo Walker
C. Butch Robins
D. Barry Mitterhoff
E. John Cowan

QUESTION 14

What group recorded the album *Bluegrass from the Gold Country*?

A. The Bluegrass Cardinals
B. The Topanga Express
C. The Vern Williams Band
D. Hardly Strictly Bluegrass
E. Red Hot and Gold Grass
F. Charlie Waller and Gold Country

QUESTION 15

What former member of the Blue Grass Boys was victim of a horrendous robbery/murder?

A. Lester Flatt
B. Stringbean
C. Pete Pike
D. Clyde Moody
E. Brad Keith
F. Mr. Ed

QUESTION 16

Who wrote the song "West Virginia My Home"?

A. John Prine
B. Hazel Dickens
C. Former U. S. Senator Robert Byrd
D. Russell Smith
E. Hazel and Grady Cole

QUESTION 17

Who was "Uncle Pen"?

A. A famous race horse from the early 20th century

B. The main character in "The Prisoner's Song"

C. James Vandiver

D. Lester Flatt

E. A frequent nom de plume for songwriter Harlan Howard

QUESTION 18

What was the site of Bill Monroe's bluegrass festival?

A. Culpeper, Virginia

B. Watermelon Park, Virginia

C. Gettysburg, Pennsylvania

D. Indian Springs, Maryland

E. Bean Blossom, Indiana

F. Rosine, Kentucky

QUESTION 19

What Bill Monroe song did Elvis Presley record?

A. Big Elv
B. Rose of Old Kentucky
C. Blue Moon of Kentucky
D. Rawhide
E. Tennessee Stud
F. Love Me Tender

QUESTION 20

Can you name this musician who played in Bill Monroe's band for an uninterrupted 10 years as one of the Blue Grass Boys?

A. Jimmy Martin
B. Lester Flatt
C. Bessie Lee Mauldin
D. Howdy Forrester
E. Kenny Baker
F. Cleo Davis

QUESTION 21

Who was the only person to play the accordion as a member of the Blue Grass Boys?

A. Clyde Moody
B. Wilene Forrester
C. Merle "Red" Taylor
D. Joel Price
E. Bill "Cousin Wilbur" Wesbrooks

QUESTION 22

To Bill Monroe, where did the fiddle begin?

A. Rosine
B. Bean Blossom
C. Jenny Lynn
D. Culpeper, Virginia
E. Salt Creek

QUESTION 23

With Bill Monroe the Father of Bluegrass Music, what did that make James Monroe?

    A.   His guitar player

    B.   The son of bluegrass music

    C.   Bluegrass Music

    D.   The bass player in the band

    E.   A recording star in his own right

QUESTION 24

If Bill Monroe is the Father of Bluegrass Music, who is the son of Bluegrass Music?

QUESTION 25

Granted that Monroe is the Father of Bluegrass Music, who is the Father of Country Music?

- A.   Hank Williams
- B.   Roy Acuff
- C.   Jimmie Rodgers
- D.   Uncle Dave Macon
- E.   Hank Snow

QUESTION 26

Who of the following was a notable Native American bluegrass musician?

- A.   Cedric Rainwater
- B.   Chief Powhatan
- C.   Dudley Connell
- D.   Frank Necessary
- E.   Natchez the Indian

QUESTION 27

What was Del McCoury's main instrument before he joined the Blue Grass Boys?

QUESTION 28

Which bluegrass singer, who Bob Dylan once called "the country Stevie Wonder" was best known for the song "At the End of A Long Lonely Day"?

    A.   Marty Robbins

    B.   Doc Watson

    C.   Russell Moore

    D.   Jim Eanes

    E.   John Herald

QUESTION 29

Which bluegrass record label spelled its name backwards?

    A.   Leber

    B.   Vetco

    C.   County

    D.   Marietta

    E.   Revonah

    F.   Ahura Mazda

Bonus points if you know why.

QUESTION 30

You say you've got a pig at home in a pen and corn to feed him on? Many people would say it's kind of obvious that you only lack one thing to make your life complete. What is that one thing you still need in life?

QUESTION 31

Which band was the first to perform bluegrass music at the White House?

- A. The Osborne Brothers
- B. Alison Krauss and Union Station
- C. II Generation
- D. The Country Gentlemen
- E. The Johnson Mountain Boys

QUESTION 32

Which bluegrass group was the first to play Carnegie Hall?

- A. Roy Hall and his Blue Ridge Entertainers
- B. Lester Flatt and Earl Scruggs
- C. Earl Taylor and the Stony Mountain Boys
- D. The Kentucky Colonels
- E. The Greenbriar Boys

QUESTION 33

Which one of the following things was once found on Rocky Top?

    A.   Smoggy smoke

    B.   A telephone bill

    C.   A girl who was half-bear and the other half cat

    D.   Corn

    E.   An old-time banjo man

QUESTION 34

Who played bass on all but one of the albums of the Bluegrass Album Band?

    A.   Marshall Wilborn

    B.   Lynn Morris

    C.   Bob Tidwell

    D.   Todd Phillips

    E.   Tom Gray

QUESTION 35

Which of the following is Drusilla Adams most associated with?

    A.   Her son, banjo player Tom Adams

    B.   Blue Ridge Records

    C.   Porter Church

    D.   The song "Little Old Cabin in the Lane"

    E.   The Addams Family Band

QUESTION 36

Who is the composer of "Jesus Loves His Mandolin Player #16"?

    A. David Grisman

    B. Andy Statman

    C. Becky Smith

    D. Jethro Burns

    E. Frank Wakefield

QUESTION 37

True or false: Doc Watson performed at the 1968 Olympic Games, the same games at which two American athletes gave the clenched-fist "black power" salute after receiving their medals?

QUESTION 38

What bluegrass musician's death prompted the Governor of the state to call out the Tennessee National Guard?

A. Ray Brewster

B. Red Allen

C. Charlie Cline

D. Dave Akeman

E. Bill Monroe

QUESTION 39

What bluegrass group had Martha White's self-rising flour in mind at the time the group was formed?

A. Lester Flatt and Nashville Grass
B. Hot Rize
C. Rhonda Vincent
D. Del McCoury and the Dixie Pals
E. Breakfast Special

QUESTION 40

What early Rounder Records recording artist later became a prominent bluegrass businessperson?

A. Barry Poss
B. George Pegram
C. Nancy Talbott
D. Steve Harris
E. Chris Jones

QUESTION 41

What Columbia Records recording group led directly to the founding of the group Up with People?

    A.   Jim and Jesse
    B.   The Stanley Brothers
    C.   The Colwell Brothers
    D.   The Bluegrass Alliance
    E.   Doyle Lawson and Quicksilver

QUESTION 42

Which of these bands never had a female as part of the band?

    A.   Jimmy Martin and the Sunny Mountain Boys
    B.   Bill Monroe and His Blue Grass Boys
    C.   Lester Flatt, Earl Scruggs and the Foggy Mountain Boys
    D.   Blue Rose
    E.   Dry Branch Fire Squad

QUESTION 43

When he wandered again to his home in the mountains, where in youth's early dawn he was happy and free, who or what did the singer encounter?

A. The man who murdered Omie Wise
B. Uncle Pen
C. Rank strangers
D. The Lord
E. His long-lost brother
F. A pig in a pen

QUESTION 44

What mountain music song features the line "the willows will hang their heads"?

A. Bury Me Beneath the Willow
B. White Dove
C. Down in the Willow Garden
D. Poor Willie
E. Good Ole Mountain Dew

QUESTION 45

What bluegrass or mountain music song features an after-death visitation?

- A. Rocky Top
- B. Fox on the Run
- C. Bringing Mary Home
- D. Oh Death
- E. The Drunken Driver

QUESTION 46

While the women's all a-laughing, the children all a-crying, and the men all a-hollering, what else was going on?

Vintage photograph from Union Grove

QUESTION 47

What musician recorded with the Rolling Stones, appeared on *Star Trek*, was in the movie *Basic Instinct*, and also worked as a Blue Grass Boy?

    A.   Ry Cooder

    B.   Dan Crary

    C.   John Hickman

    D.   Lamar Grier

    E.   Byron Berline

    F.   Scotty Stoneman

QUESTION 48

What was the name of the family band in which Rhonda Vincent and Darrin Vincent were raised?

A.   The American Bluegrass Express
B.   The Sally Mountain Show
C.   The McLain Family Band
D.   Dailey and Vincent
E.   The II Generation

QUESTION 49

Which brother duet lasted longer than any other in the field of bluegrass or country music?

A.   The Whitstein Brothers
B.   The Louvin Brothers
C.   The Delmore Brothers
D.   Del and Jerry McCoury
E.   Jim and Jesse

QUESTION 50

Which bluegrass musician went on to form a record company notable in the field?

- A. Fred Bartenstein
- B. Ken Irwin
- C. Alison Brown
- D. Jimmie Skinner
- E. Jim Lauderdale

QUESTION 51

What was the band name most associated with Reno and Smiley's work?

- A. Tommy Magness and the Tennessee Buddies
- B. Toby Stroud's Miles of Smiles
- C. The Tennessee Cut-Ups
- D. Fire on the Mountain
- E. The Highwoods Stringband

QUESTION 52

What was Tater Tate's given first name?

    A.   Thomas

    B.   Clarence

    C.   Wilson

    D.   Harold

    E.   Austin

    F.   That was it—he was named Tater

QUESTION 53

In what state did the Lilly Brothers have enduring success?

    A.   West Virginia

    B.   Massachusetts

    C.   California

    D.   North Carolina

    E.   Tennessee

QUESTION 54

Who of the following was not at least an occasional member of the Lilly Brothers band?

A. Tex Logan
B. Herb Hooven
C. Eli Lilly
D. Don Stover
E. Joe Val

QUESTION 55

Which singer or musician had 22 brothers and sisters?

A. Little Roy Lewis
B. Jere Cherryholmes
C. Wilma Lee Cooper
D. Margie Sullivan
E. Scotty Stoneman

QUESTION 56

Who is the only one of the following men named Monroe who was once part of the Blue Grass Boys?

    A. John

    B. Harry

    C. Speed

    D. Birch

    E. Charlie

QUESTION 57

Who decided to start a record company when Charlie Bailey and His Happy Valley Boys were snowed in at his home in Westbrook, Maine back in 1955?

A. Chris Strachwitz

B. Al Hawkes

C. Dave Freeman

D. Carl Story

E. Bob French

Jesse McReynolds and band, 2014.

QUESTION 58

What did President William McKinley do right after he was struck by an assassin's bullet?

    A.   Prayed for America

    B.   Died

    C.   Hollered and squalled

    D.   Pulled out an Ivor-Johnson gun

    E.   Cashed in his checks

Courtesy of Library of Congress

QUESTION 59

When Bill Monroe's 1939 rendition of "Mule Skinner Blues" reportedly earned the first encore ever at the Grand Ole Opry, what instrument was he playing?

    A.   None. He only sang vocals on the song at the time.

    B.   Guitar

    C.   Mandolin

    D.   Bass

    E.   Fiddle

QUESTION 60

Which are almost certainly the most famous set of twins in bluegrass music?

    A.   Jim & Jesse McReynolds

    B.   The Delmore Brothers

    C.   The Shankmans

    D.   The Bailes Brothers

    E.   Jimmy and Benny Martin

QUESTION 61

Which of these was not a Jimmy Martin album title?

    A.   Free Born Man

    B.   The Last Song

    C.   Tennessee

    D.   I'd Like to be Sixteen Again

    E.   Sunny Side of the Mountain

Jimmy Martin, King of Bluegrass

QUESTION 62

Which popular or rock artist or group has not yet had a bluegrass album devoted to his or their music? Which was the first to inspire a tribute album?

A. Chuck Berry
B. The Moody Blues
C. The Grateful Dead
D. The Rolling Stones
E. The Beatles

QUESTION 63

True or false: Benny Martin was once managed by Col. Tom Parker and opened almost three dozen dates for Elvis Presley?

QUESTION 64

Which lead vocalist comes to mind when you think of the TV show, *The Beverly Hillbillies*?

- A. Carl Story
- B. Jim Eanes
- C. Lester Flatt
- D. Jed Clampett
- E. Buddy Ebsen

QUESTION 65

Which bluegrass or country singer or group used to also bring his own baseball team on tour with him?

- A. Bill Monroe
- B. Chuck Connors
- C. Danny and Charlie, the Bailey Brothers
- D. Roy Acuff
- E. Red Belcher

QUESTION 66

Who was never a member of the Newgrass Revival?

A. Courtney Johnson
B. Bela Fleck
C. Curtis Burch
D. Pat Enright
E. Pat Flynn
F. Kimber Ludiker

QUESTION 67

True or false: Curly Ray Cline was the ex-mayor of Norton, Virginia.

QUESTION 68

Who, among the following five, was the first to be a member of J. D. Crowe's band?

- A.   Tony Rice
- B.   Larry Rice
- C.   Ron Rice
- D.   Wyatt Rice
- E.   Herb Rice

QUESTION 69

When Bill Keith joined the Blue Grass Boys, the leader of the band didn't want another Bill in the band so he became Brad Keith. Which of the following similarly changed his or her name when joining a band?

- A.   John Duffey
- B.   Joe Meadows
- C.   Alison Brown
- D.   Carl Jackson
- E.   Charlie Moore

QUESTION 70

What does the "D" in J. D. Crowe stand for?

    A. Donald
    B. It's just an initial
    C. Dee
    D. Daniel
    E. Darnell

QUESTION 71

Who was the first lead singer in the Clinch Mountain Boys after Carter Stanley's death?

A.   Charlie Sizemore

B.   Herschel Sizemore

C.   Roy Lee Centers

D.   Ralph Stanley II

E.   Larry Sparks

QUESTION 72

Which of the following songs does not have a murder in it?

A.   Down in the Willow Garden

B.   Omie Wise

C.   Poor Ellen Smith

D.   Banks of the Ohio

E.   Little Girl and the Dreadful Snake

QUESTION 73

Who was the founder of Alison Krauss's band Union Station?

    A. Alison Krauss

    B. Tim Stafford

    C. Andrea Zonn

    D. brother Viktor Krauss

    E. John Pennell

QUESTION 74

Which musician spent many years playing in an official United States Navy bluegrass band?

    A. Bill Waldron

    B. Bill Keith

    C. Bill Emerson

    D. Bill Bailey

    E. Bill Wooten

    F. Bill Vernon

QUESTION 75

Which of the following was the oldest before becoming a member of the Grand Ole Opry?

    A. Bill Monroe

    B. Grandpa Jones

    C. Stoney Cooper

    D. Little Jimmy Dickens

    E. Ralph Stanley

QUESTION 76

Who wrote "In the Good Old Days (When Times Were Bad)"?

    A. Adam Steffey

    B. Paul Williams

    C. Leona Helmsley

    D. Dolly Parton

    E. Carter Stanley

    F. Sharon McGraw

QUESTION 77

Which of the following was NOT a pseudonym used by Bill
Monroe as a songwriter?

    A.   Wilbur Jones

    B.   Albert Price

    C.   Joe Ahr

    D.   James B. Smith

    E.   Arnold Birch

QUESTION 78

Which musician was not a member of the Bluegrass Alliance?

    A.   Jerry Douglas

    B.   Tony Rice

    C.   Vince Gill

    D.   Sam Bush

    E.   Dan Crary

QUESTION 79

Each of the following bluegrass bands appeared one or more times on TV sitcoms, as themselves or under fictional names—except one. Which one did not?

    A.   The Dillards

    B.   Flatt & Scruggs

    C.   The Kentucky Colonels

    D.   The Darlings

    E.   Jimmy Martin & the Sunny Mountain Boys

QUESTION 80

True or false: After he suffered a near-fatal car wreck, Don Reno wrote a song called "I'm Using My Bible for a Road Map."

QUESTION 81

Who was the first president of the International Bluegrass Music Association?

A. Katy Daley

B. Art Menius

C. Gabrielle Gray

D. Dan Hays

E. Pete Wernick

F. Della Mae

G. Walt Saunders

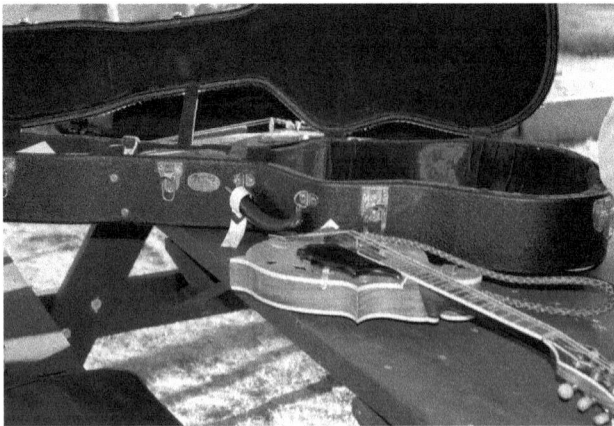

QUESTION 82

Who holds the largest number of IBMA Awards for Banjo
Player of the Year?

    A.   Jim Mills

    B.   J. D. Crowe

    C.   Ralph Stanley

    D.   Terry Baucom

    E.   Kristin Scott Benson

QUESTION 83

Who holds the most IBMA Awards as Fiddle Player of the
Year?

    A.   Stuart Duncan

    B.   Michael Cleveland

    C.   Jason Carter

    D.   Ronnie Stewart

    E.   Alison Krauss

QUESTION 84

Who holds the most IBMA Awards as instrumentalist in the Dobro category?

    A.   Josh Graves

    B.   Jerry Douglas

    C.   Rob Ickes

    D.   Bashful Brother Oswald

    E.   Phil Ledbetter

QUESTION 85

Which mandolinist has won the most IBMA Awards for work on his or her instrument?

    A.   Bill Monroe

    B.   Sierra Hull

    C.   Rhonda Vincent

    D.   Ronnie McCoury

    E.   Adam Steffey

QUESTION 86

Name the fiddler who was never a member of the Blue Grass Boys.

    A.   Buddy Spicher

    B.   Tater Tate

    C.   Richard Greene

    D.   Vassar Clements

    E.   Tex Logan

QUESTION 87

Earlier, we talked about Bill Monroe's practice for several years of carrying the Bluegrass All-Stars baseball team with him when his show was on tour. There was another William S. Monroe in baseball, a Negro Leagues infielder of some renown. True or false?

QUESTION 88

"Say, mister, where does this road go?" "It never goes anywhere. It's always there when I git up in the morning." Who was the original Arkansas Traveler?

    A.   Mike Huckabee

    B.   Jimmie Driftwood

    C.   Jim Smoak

    D.   Noah Crase

    E.   None of the above

QUESTION 89

This group used to sell flyswatters at its merchandise table. Name the group.

    A.   Dry Branch Fire Squad

    B.   The Dillards

    C.   The Lewis Family

    D.   Hot Mud Family

    E.   Hot Rize

QUESTION 90

Who was the author of "High On A Mountain"?

- A. Carter Stanley
- B. Ola Belle Reed
- C. Del McCoury
- D. Udell McPeak
- E. Curly Seckler

QUESTION 91

True or false: David Grisman's father was a professional trumpet player, and some of David's first recordings were with Red Allen, Frank Wakefield, and the Kentuckians.

QUESTION 92

Which group is considered to be the first to ever perform to a college audience?

    A. Lester Flatt and Earl Scruggs and the Foggy Mountain Boys

    B. The Osborne Brothers

    C. Country Cooking

    D. Dr. Ralph Stanley

    E. The Pinnacle Boys

QUESTION 93

True or false: Both Jamie Dailey and Darrin Vincent have been singing bluegrass since the age of three years old?

QUESTION 94

What is the name of the boy who sells the morning papers?

- A. James King
- B. Brad Keith
- C. David Grisman
- D. Luke Bulla
- E. Jimmy Brown
- F. Kyle Cantrell

QUESTION 95

Who is well-known as "the singing voice of George Clooney"?

- A. Barry Bales
- B. Ron Block
- C. Jerry Douglas
- D. Al Krauss
- E. Dan Tyminski

QUESTION 96

True or false: As a child in growing up in Pigeon Forge or Sevierville in East Tennessee, Dolly Parton was briefly a member of a family band called The Tennessee Partoners.

QUESTION 97

What work did Joe Val do for his day job?

- A. Instrument repair
- B. Railroad conductor
- C. Pharmacist
- D. Typewriter repairman
- E. Schoolteacher
- F. Writer of greeting card texts

For 31 years as of 2016, the Boston Bluegrass Union had staged a Joe Val Bluegrass Festival in Joe's honor.

QUESTION 98

What was the name of the first album to win the Grammy for Best Bluegrass Recording?

   A.   *I've Got That Old Feeling* by Alison Krauss
   B.   *Southern Flavor* by Bill Monroe
   C.   *Bluegrass Rules* by Ricky Skaggs
   D.   *Every Time You Say Goodbye* by Alison Krauss
   E.   *Uncle Pen* by Bill Monroe

QUESTION 99

This musician played his or her instrument during brain surgery. Who is he/she?

   A.   Roger Frisch
   B.   John Duffey
   C.   Sam Bush
   D.   Eddie Adcock
   E.   Missy Raines
   F.   Frank Wakefield

QUESTION 100

Which bluegrass musician was tragically killed while loading equipment into the back of his car?

A.   Bea Lilly

B.   Ray Brewster

C.   Clarence White

D.   Buzz Busby

E.   Carter Stanley

QUESTION 101

True or false: J.D. Crowe first broke into bluegrass with Jimmy Martin and the Sunny Mountain Boys.

QUESTION 102

One of the most popular bands of the 1980s was the traditional bluegrass band, the Johnson Mountain Boys. In what state was the Johnson Mountain they named the group after located?

A. Georgia

B. Utah

C. West Virginia

D. It's not actually located in a state; it's in the District of Columbia.

E. They just made up the name because it sounded good.

The first JMB album, known affectionately in some circles as "0135."

QUESTION 103

Who paid $1,000,000 or more to buy Bill Monroe's mandolin after his death?

    A.   Ricky Skaggs

    B.   No one; it was smashed by intruders who broke into his home.

    C.   The Bill Monroe Foundation

    D.   James Pendleton Vandiver

    E.   John Paul Jones

QUESTION 104

What was the name of Jim Stanton's record label?

    A.   Revonah

    B.   Webco

    C.   Blue Ridge

    D.   Rich-R-Tone

    E.   Canary

QUESTION 105

The same old man is living at the mill and the mill turns around of its own free will. Where are the old man's hands?

- A. On his fiddle and bow
- B. They were both amputated when he was hit by a drunken driver
- C. Around his true love's neck
- D. One in the hopper and the other in the sack
- E. Stiff and arthritic, old, and only in the way

QUESTION 106

True or false: All three of these musicians joined the bands in question at age 14: Ricky Skaggs and Keith Whitley, when joining Ralph Stanley, and Carl Jackson, when joining Jim & Jesse.

QUESTION 107

You can read it in the morning papers, hear it on the radio. Crime is sweeping the nation. This world is about to go. What does the world need?

QUESTION 108

Which of the following are inductees in the Country Music Hall of Fame, and the Nashville Songwriters Hall of Fame, and the Rock and Roll Hall of Fame?

   A.   Bill Monroe
   B.   Hank Williams
   C.   Johnny Cash
   D.   Jimmie Rodgers
   E.   Bob Wills

QUESTION 109

Who was the first bluegrass artist or group to sell 1,000,000 copies of a given album?

    A.   The Nitty Gritty Dirt Band

    B.   Flatt & Scruggs

    C.   Eric Weissberg

    D.   Nickel Creek

    E.   Alison Krauss & Union Station

QUESTION 110

Which former Blue Grass Boy served the longest stint as Bill's lead singer?

    A.   Wayne Lewis

    B.   Jimmy Martin

    C.   Lester Flatt

    D.   Peter Rowan

    E.   Clyde Moody

QUESTION 111

True or false: Mac Wiseman was an active skydiver for more than 10 years.

QUESTION 112

Which group used to sell baseball caps which promoted the Kentucky School of Knife Fighting?

    A.   Ricky Skaggs and Kentucky Thunder

    B.   Dry Branch Fire Squad

    C.   Red Allen and the Kentuckians

    D.   The Shenandoah Valley Quartet

    E.   Newgrass Revival

QUESTION 113

Who was the bluegrass musician who worked for a while as a plumber at the Kennedy Space Center in Florida?

QUESTION 114

Who was the youngest person ever to become a member of the Grand Ole Opry?

A. Little Jimmy Dickens
B. Alison Krauss
C. Carol Lee Cooper
D. Ricky Skaggs
E. Mark O'Connor

QUESTION 115

What did former bass player Ebo Walker do for many years since leaving bluegrass?

Jesse McReynolds, hands at work.

QUESTION 116

True or false: There are two Monroes included in the Hollywood Walk of Fame. One is film star Marilyn Monroe. The other is a recording artist—Bill Monroe.

QUESTION 117

Which two musicians from the following list worked as writers for the Smothers Brothers TV show?

A. Ron Thomason
B. Melvin Goins
C. John Hartford
D. Steve Martin
E. Lonnie Peerce

QUESTION 118

Which of this list of artists did not record their first album for Rounder when they were 14 or younger?

A. Mark O'Connor
B. Alison Krauss
C. The Bullas
D. George Pegram
E. Sierra Hull

QUESTION 119

True or false: Jerry Garcia of The Grateful Dead once came east to audition as a member of Bill Monroe's Blue Grass Boys.

QUESTION 120

Who was the first editor of *Muleskinner News*?

   A.   Birch Monroe
   B.   Neil Rosenberg
   C.   Dick Spottswood
   D.   Fred Bartenstein
   E.   Kathy Kaplan

QUESTION 121

True or false: The deputy sheriff convicted of killing Roy Lee Centers was sentenced to 12 years in prison but let out after three months.

QUESTION 122

Which bluegrass musician was French-Canadian, born in Madawaska, Maine?

- A. Carlos Brock
- B. Simon St. Pierre
- C. French Carpenter
- D. Roland White
- E. Ned Luberecki
- F. Bob French

QUESTION 123

Can you name a father and son, each of whom has made albums under his own name for Rounder?

QUESTION 124

Can you name the musician who first recorded for Rounder in 1971, and then (nearly 40 years later) produced Steve Martin's *Rare Bird Alert*?

QUESTION 125

Who of the following artists made a bluegrass Christmas album?

    A.   Claire Lynch

    B.   NewFound Road

    C.   Bobby Hicks

    D.   David Grisman

    E.   Ted Lundy

QUESTION 126

Who is the musician who appeared on both of Hazel Dickens first two solo albums?

A. Pig Robbins

B. Dudley Connell

C. Jerry Douglas

D. Norman Blake

E. Scott Billington

HAZEL DICKENS

Hard Hitting Songs for Hard Hit People

QUESTION 127

Which bluegrass artist is also known as a member of the bar?

- A. Keith Whitley
- B. Charlie Sizemore
- C. Joe Diffie
- D. Art Menius
- E. Roy Lee Centers
- F. Ray Goins

QUESTION 128

The soundtrack album to the movie *O Brother Where Are Thou?* was a monster hit, probably even more so than the film itself. It inspired at least one followup album, which was itself perhaps the best-selling bluegrass album a year later. Can you name the followup album?

QUESTION 129

Can you name the band currently active in 2015 whose banjo player is directly related to Arval Hogan of both Whitey and Hogan and of The Briarhoppers?

QUESTION 130

Which bluegrass personality was born in Big Spraddle Creek (near Stratton), Virginia?

- A. Alecia Nugent
- B. Ralph Stanley
- C. Sidney Cox
- D. Jim Eanes
- E. Bill Clifton

QUESTION 131

Who of the following lived to be over 100 years old?

A. Wade Mainer

B. J. E. Mainer

C. Wiley Morris

D. Pop Stoneman

E. Uncle Dave Macon

QUESTION 132

Can you name the band most closely associated with Tim Stafford?

QUESTION 133

When you hear the names Evelyn, Lynn, Sidney, Suzanne, and Willard, what group name comes to mind?

QUESTION 134

Back at question #102, you learned that there really isn't a Johnson Mountain after which the Johnson Mountain Boys were named. Let's consider the Charles River Valley Boys. Was there a Charles River, and—if so—who was the river itself named after?

QUESTION 135

What instrument in a bluegrass band means "good" in the Slovak language?

QUESTION 136

Can you name the man (he died in 1943) whose musical instruments typically sell in the $175,000 - $250,000 range, when one is made available for sale?

QUESTION 137

What is the name of the acclaimed bluegrass documentary film made by director Rachel Liebling?

    A.   *High Lonesome*

    B.   *Keep Your Skillet Good and Greasy*

    C.   *Knee Deep in Bluegrass*

    D.   *I'm On My Way Back to the Old Home*

    E.   *True Life Blues*

QUESTION 138

When bluegrass radio host Katy Daley interviews the leader of The Rage on her www.bluegrasscountry.org morning radio show, what has she inadvertently created?

QUESTION 139

What noted musician goes by the nickname "Flux"?

QUESTION 140

Whose first album was "dedicated to the staff of the Columbia Middle School"?

QUESTION 141

What is the later, and better-known, name of the group first known as the Country Boys?

QUESTION 142

Can you name the author of the song "Things in Life"?

QUESTION 143

Can you name the author of the song "Don't Put Her Down, You Helped Put Her There"?

QUESTION 144

It may not be a warhorse—not a bluegrass standard—but can you name the writer of "George and Gladys Kazatski"?

QUESTION 145

True or false: Jerry Douglas played on the very first album by Alison Krauss.

QUESTION 146

After the Carroll County accident, what was in the little box circled by a rubber band which was found behind the dash of Mary's crumpled-up machine?

QUESTION 147

What song contains the lyric "You're doing all the pitching and the game is in your hands"?

Pickers at the Union Grove Fiddlers Convention ca. 1966. That makes it pre-Rounder!

QUESTION 148

Pretty much everyone knows that Lester Flatt and Earl Scruggs were both in Bill Monroe's band before going out on their own. Were either of the Stanley Brothers also in the Blue Grass Boys?

QUESTION 149

Bluegrass Routes — a fun bluegrass trivia board game — says that this man played mandolin for the Stanley Brothers, played guitar for the Lonesome Pine Fiddlers, and played banjo for Jim & Jesse — all by the age of 19. Can you name him?

QUESTION 150

While giving a nod to Bluegrass Routes, the game also asks which member of The Grascals once played "Viva Viagra" in a band during a TV commercial for the product. Who was it?

QUESTION 151

How many Grammys were won by the Stanley Brothers?

QUESTION 152

What band was inadvertently featured on festival posters in letters twice as big as headliners such as Bill Monroe?

Pickers someplace else.

QUESTION 153

Look a-yonder comin'—what was the Orange Blossom
Special actually doing?

QUESTION 154

Who was the oldest member of the group Old and in the
Way?

QUESTION 155

True or false: Art Stamper played fiddle for every one of these groups: The Goins Brothers, Jim & Jesse, Bill Monroe, Larry Sparks, The Stanley Brothers.

QUESTION 156

What bluegrass band was named after a horse?

QUESTION 157

What bluegrass artist was asked to re-cut a song which seemed to feature inter-racial love?

QUESTION 158

Which bluegrass singer is most closely associated with John Deere tractors?

QUESTION 159

What member of a noted bluegrass group went on to become an executive at the Smithsonian Institution?

QUESTION 160

Name the person who was named IBMA Female Vocalist of the Year for seven years in a row? Hint: she was a woman!

QUESTION 161

Who is generally credited with establishing Bill Monroe as the "Father of Bluegrass Music"?

QUESTION 162

When Willie saw Molly dancing at a bar, a jealous thought came to his mind, and he said to himself, "I'll kill that girl, my own true lover
Before I let another man beat my time." Did he do it? If so, how did he do it? And who tells us the story?

QUESTION 163

Can you name two people who were left to die like a tramp on the street?

QUESTION 164

Which one of the Byrds recorded an album for County Records while a United States Senator?

QUESTION 165

Which Nashville band, founded by Mike Henderson, provided much of the music for the film *Get Low*?

Yes, it's a Rounder album.

QUESTION 166

What prompted Lester Flatt to develop his famous "G-run"?

QUESTION 167

Which of the following radio stations did not have the associated slogan? Note: there could be more than one.

A. Raleigh's WPTF "We Protect the Family"
B. Asheville's WWNC "Wonderful Western North Carolina"
C. Bristol's WCYB "We Cover You Best"
D. Bristol's WOPI "Watch Our Popularity Increase"
E. Nashville's WSM "We Shield Millions"

QUESTION 168

Can you name the mandolin player whose name is indentified with the technique called "cross-picking"?

QUESTION 169

After Flatt and Scruggs left the Blue Grass Boys and started the Foggy Mountain Boys, which notable personality joined Bill's band as lead singer?

QUESTION 170

What motion picture popularized the tune we know as "Duelin' Banjos"?

QUESTION 171

Who recorded the piece "Duelin' Banjos" for the film which made it so popular?

QUESTION 172

Which bluegrass singer won an IBMA award back in 1997 with the Front Porch String Band and then another in 2010 with a self-named band?

QUESTION 173

Which of these groups was the original Cut-Ups?

    A.   Shenandoah Cut-Ups

    B.   Virginia Cut-Ups

    C.   Tennessee Cut-Ups

    D.   Bluegrass Cut-Ups

    E.   Blue Ridge Cut-Ups

QUESTION 174

What bluegrass musician owned his own nightclub?

QUESTION 175

What bluegrass musician was the first one to ever receive Boston's Berklee School of Music's prestigious Presidential Scholarship?

QUESTION 176

Them that refuse it are few. What is it?

QUESTION 177

Because another record company spread the rumor that Rounder had never paid Doc Watson any royalties, Clarence White declined to record an album for Rounder. Clarence was killed shortly afterward. Why hadn't Rounder ever paid Doc any royalties?

QUESTION 178

Who is this? He started professionally at age 14 working with Jim & Jesse, then played 12 years with Glen Campbell, and later produced the album *Livin', Lovin', Losin' — Songs Of The Louvin Brothers* which won the 2003 Grammy for Country Album of the Year.

QUESTION 179

Do you know who the bluegrass singer is who changed his name upon becoming a full-time musician so as not to embarrass his father, who was something on the order of a prominent bond salesman? His father told him, "We don't want you singing hillbilly music and using the family name. You'll have to come up with something else."

QUESTION 180

Who recorded and produced the seminal Folkways album
Mountain Music Bluegrass Style?

QUESTION 181

If you don't love your neighbor, then who else don't you love?

QUESTION 182

If you come in with your hair mussed up and your clothes
don't fit you right, and you won't tell where you've been, what
will I do?

QUESTION 183

As long as the sun goes up and comes down, and the big blue sky goes down to the ground, as long as the world goes round and round, what will I keep doing?

QUESTION 184

You were young and in your prime and you left your home in Caroline. Now your grip is packed to travel and you're scratching gravel. Where are you headed?

QUESTION 185

If you don't from sin retire, what will He do?

QUESTION 186

Who was his best pal?

> I lost a friend and a pal, boys I laid him down to rest
> I weeped and moaned over his grave and to me boys it was sad
> 'Cause I knew down beneath that mound lay the best pal I ever
> had

QUESTION 187

Sugar coated love, you gave me on a plate. I took a bite and then I looked to see what I had ate. What *had* you ate?

QUESTION 188

If you had the wings of an angel, what would you do?

QUESTION 189

Your Sophronie has left you and she's found another man. Perhaps it was your behavior that did you in? Tell us: what was your motto?

QUESTION 190

You're a free born man. Where is your home?

QUESTION 191

In Jimmy Martin's song "Truck Driving Man," what was the name of the roadhouse in Texas?

Here he is again: Jimmy Martin. Signing autographs for young admirers.

QUESTION 192

How old was Sonny Osborne when he became a Blue Grass Boy?

    A. 21
    B. 28
    C. 18
    D. 14
    E. 20

QUESTION 193

What was Sonny Osborne's first name?

QUESTION 194

Can you name the African American musician who was a major influence on Bill Monroe?

QUESTION 195

This man was called the "Jimi Hendrix of the violin" by Peter Rowan and the "bluegrass Charlie Parker" by Jerry Garcia. Who is he?

QUESTION 196

At least 25 of the Blue Grass Boys had last names which are nouns. Can you name 10 of them?

QUESTION 197

How many bluegrass personalities can you think of whose name includes a color?

QUESTION 198

What internationally famous musician told *Rolling Stone* magazine, "I'd still rather listen to Bill and Charlie Monroe than any current record"?

QUESTION 199

True or false: Lester Flatt's wife Gladys — they met as fellow workers in a textile mill — used to play in Monroe's band.

QUESTION 200

Which bluegrass musician was awarded an "honoris causa" college degree?

- A. Peter Wernick
- B. Bela Fleck
- C. Ralph Stanley
- D. Peter Rowan
- E. Buzz Busby

QUESTION 201

Which is the best among the bluegrass record labels?

- A. Rounder Records
- B. Rounder
- C. Rounder Records
- D. Rounder
- E. Deutsche Grammophon

QUESTION 202

What would you give in exchange for your soul?

QUESTION 203

True or false: Before she broke big at the Monterey Pop Festival, 1960s San Francisco-based rocker Janis Joplin played with a bluegrass band.

QUESTION 204

In the song "Long Black Veil" the slayer who ran looked a lot like the singer of the song. What had the singer done, for which he was killed?

    A.   Killed someone 'neath the town hall light

    B.   Courted Omie Wise and pushed her in deep waters where he knew that she would drown

    C.   He dug on Pretty Polly's grave the biggest part of last night

    D.   Basically, nothing at the sort.

QUESTION 205

Which of these acts was an immediate success in 2014, faithfully working with repertoire from the middle 1950s?

A. The Earls of Leicester
B. The Harrells of Reno
C. The Boxcars
D. Vern & Ray

QUESTION 206

Which Alison also runs a record label, and which label?

A. Alison Krauss
B. Alison Brown
C. Alison Wonderland
D. Alison Lundergan Grimes

QUESTION 207

Which noted musician is named after not one, not two, but three classical music composers, each one from a different country?

QUESTION 208

True or false: the Newgrass Revival was formed more than 40 years ago?

QUESTION 209

Fans of the music know Bill Monroe as the "Father of Blue Grass Music" and James Monroe as "The Son of the Father of Blue Grass Music," but who was called "The Father of Bluegrass Gospel Music"?

QUESTION 210

Which member of a British rock group produced an album by Uncle Earl?

    A.   Brian Jones

    B.   John Paul Jones

    C.   Robert Plant

    D.   George Harrison

    E.   Roger Daltrey

Part of the crowd at Thomas Point Beach, Maine, 2014.

QUESTION 211

Speaking of Uncle Earl, which of the following musicians was not in the band?

A. Abigail Washburn
B. Casey Henry
C. Earl Taylor
D. Tahmineh Gueramy
E. Earl Scruggs

QUESTION 212

Ricky Skaggs has recorded albums with several other musicians. Who among these were not album collaborators with him?

A. Bruce Hornsby
B. Tony Rice
C. Sharon White
D. Keith Whitley
E. Bill Monroe

QUESTION 213

What is the relationship between Little Roy Lewis, Polly Lewis, and Laurie Lewis?

QUESTION 214

What notable couple's child shares something in common with the Canadian Academy of Recording Arts and Sciences?

QUESTION 215

What might one say the following artists have in common?

A. Kenny and Amanda Smith
B. Vassar Clements
C. Harley Allen
D. Hunter Berry
E. Carl Jackson
F. Tony Rice
G. Kenny Baker

QUESTION 216

The Gibson Brothers won back-to-back IBMA Entertainer of the Year Awards in 2012 and 2013. Which of these groups won three or more consecutive awards in the category?

    A.   Alison Krauss

    B.   Del McCoury

    C.   Dailey and Vincent

    D.   The Nashville Bluegrass Band

    E.   The Grascals

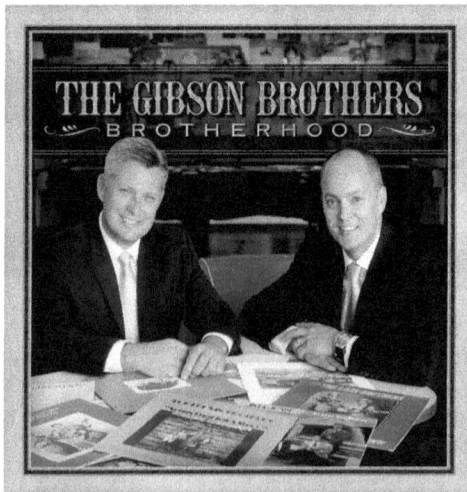

The Gibson Brothers album cover cleverly depicts covers of other Rounder albums featuring brother duets.

QUESTION 217

It's easy to understand why the Stanley Brothers' band was named the Clinch Mountain Boys, but with some other bands, it can a little more difficult to pin down. What is the geographic distance between Johnson Mountain and Steep Canyon?

QUESTION 218

Two of the most prolific songwriters in bluegrass music were Certain and Stacey, who combined efforts were frequently recorded by Lester Flatt and Earl Scruggs and the Foggy Mountain Boys. Who were these guys and were they members of the band?

QUESTION 219

If you were to have just a little talk with Jesus, what might you do?

    A. Tell Him all about our troubles

    B. Ask Him to keep you on the way

    C. Talk about Little Moses

    D. Confess your sins and ask forgiveness

QUESTION 220

The resonator guitar called the Dobro got its name from:

    A. The parent company of Martha White Flour

    B. Two Slovak Americans named John and Emil Dopyera

    C. Bashful Brother Oswald's famous line, "Show me the dough, bro!"

    D. Jerry "Flux" Douglas

QUESTION 221

Everyone knows bluegrass has a lot of songs about mother and death. But one famous song says Mother's not dead. What is she doing?

    A.   She's baking Martha White biscuits

    B.   She's comforting her children, to keep them from fear

    C.   She's only a-sleeping

    D.   She's out on the town, building a bad reputation

QUESTION 222

"Love 'em and leave 'em, kiss 'em and grieve 'em." That used to be his motto so high. What happened to transform this male singer's approach to relationships?

    A.   He became a man of constant sorrow

    B.   The murder of Omie Wise

    C.   Sensitivity workshops at IBMA

    D.   Sophronie

QUESTION 223

Bluegrass can sometimes offer personal advice. If you find a big rock in the road — and if you favor shady dealing — what warning should you keep in mind?

QUESTION 224

Bill Monroe said this world was not his home, but also that he was sitting on top of the world. Nothing wrong with that logic. Many of his song titles referenced actual places in the world, e.g., "Brown County Blues." Leaving aside places such as Heaven, what are the only two geographic places outside the Unites States that he specifically mentioned in a song title?

QUESTION 225

Bill Monroe mentioned places such as Louisville, Roanoke, Brooklyn, Kansas City, and Ashland in his song titles—even Columbus ("Columbus Stockade.") Can you name the three state capitals he mentioned in a song title?

QUESTION 226

Monroe mentioned state names in at least 25 song titles. There are nine states that he mentioned. Can you identify the state which he named most frequently? (This is not necessarily a trick question.)

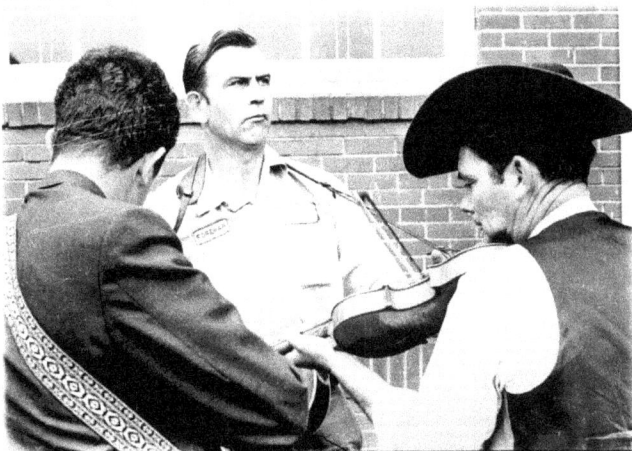

More pickin' outside the school at Union Grove.

QUESTION 227

Can you name the state(s) that came in second? Just to provide a little help, the nine states he mentioned are: Alabama, California, Georgia, Louisiana, Kentucky, Ohio, Tennessee, Texas, and Virginia.

QUESTION 228

Borderline sacrilege? No offense intended. What bluegrass song contains something of a reference to what could be called arson?

QUESTION 229

OK, so Bill Monroe once mentioned Ernest Tubb in a song. Can you name the bluegrass song in which the lyrics mention by name every single member of an unrelated band?

QUESTION 230

A broken heart will keep on crying. What song contains those words?

QUESTION 231

Speaking of broken hearts, there's a song with these two lines:

A. I knew you were no good right from the start
My friends all told me you'd break my heart

B. The singer says he (or she) is not living. No, not a ghost. How does the singer explain his or her status?

QUESTION 232

Who prayed every morning, noon, and night?

QUESTION 233

Can you name the song that starts with this line?

Two strikes against me before I even start

QUESTION 234

What song was written by the late, great fiddler Tex Logan?

- A. "Big Sandy River"
- B. "Christmas Time's A-Comin'"
- C. "All Alone in the Lone Star State"
- D. "Katy Hill"

QUESTION 235

Don Reno's first name was actually Don (not Donald). What was Red Smiley's first name?

QUESTION 236

Speaking of Reno and Smiley, this classic bluegrass duo traveled a great deal over the 15 years of their career. One of their first songs was "There's Another Baby Waiting for Me Down the Line," cut for King Records in 1952. What did they use for a roadmap?

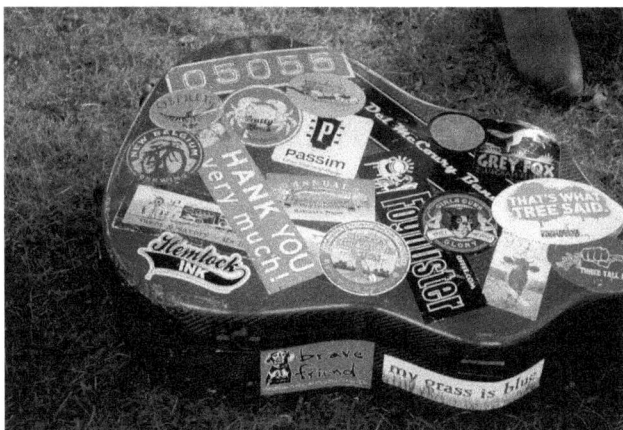

QUESTION 237

If your garments are spotless and white as snow, what might they have been washed in?

    A. blood

    B. Martha White's self-rising flour

    C. soft soap

    D. red clay

QUESTION 238

Let's say you're in a relationship with another person and that person tells you she's sick of your house and to get off the couch, asks you where in the hell you have been, looks at you like she might hate you, and says you need a new attitude, what might be the remedy?

QUESTION 239

When you think of the meanest lady cop in East Kentucky, who first comes to mind?

    A.   Dale Ann Bradley

    B.   Minnie Pearl

    C.   Charlie Sizemore

    D.   Louise Scruggs

    E.   Thelma Louise Parker

QUESTION 240

Name the scholar or musician who once described bluegrass as "blues and jazz"—or, more completely: "Scottish bagpipes and ole-time fiddlin'. It's Methodist and Holiness and Baptist. It's blues and jazz, and it has a high lonesome sound."

QUESTION 241

People buy recordings of bluegrass for a number of reasons –
usually because they've heard a track or two off the album, or
seen the artist in person. People might discuss albums as, for
instance, "the Old and in the Way album," but often people
could never even name the label on which the album was
issued. There is one particular recording which was always
known not even necessarily by the record label's name, but by
its catalog number. How many people know that *Bill Monroe's
Country Music Hall of Fame* album was Decca DL75281?
Well, people know *this* album by its catalog number. What
album is it?

QUESTION 242

What musician changed his stage name when he joined
Lester Flatt and Earl Scruggs, and what was his stage name
before joining their band?

QUESTION 243

Can you name the bluegrass song in which the singer sings, "If I don't see her soon, I think I will explode"?

QUESTION 244

Can you name the bluegrass group that recorded the song "You Can't Make A Heel Toe the Mark"?

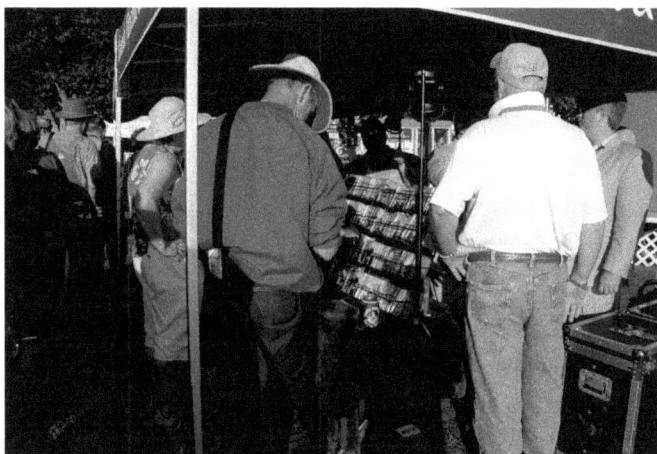

Browsing the wares at the Thomas Point Beach festival.

QUESTION 245

Billy Mack was buried under 20 tons of steel by a widow maker. Who was the woman he had left behind?

A. Wilma Walker
B. Wanda Anne
C. Ruby
D. Della Mae
E. Bessie Lee

The group named Della Mae.

QUESTION 246

Which group performs a song, written by a member of the group, which contains the line: "You're the best son that I never had"?

QUESTION 247

Is it true that the Dillards once fired longtime WAMU-FM bluegrass disc jockey Gary Henderson—for playing too much bluegrass? Gary has been on the air since 1967, so this firing occurred even before that.

QUESTION 248

Which one of these TV shows or movies featured bluegrass the least? To qualify, the show/film had to feature the music somewhat.

A. *Beverly Hillbillies*

B. *Hee Haw*

C. *Deliverance*

D. *Justified*

E. *Andy Griffith Show*

F. *Bonnie & Clyde*

G. *O Brother, Where Art Thou?*

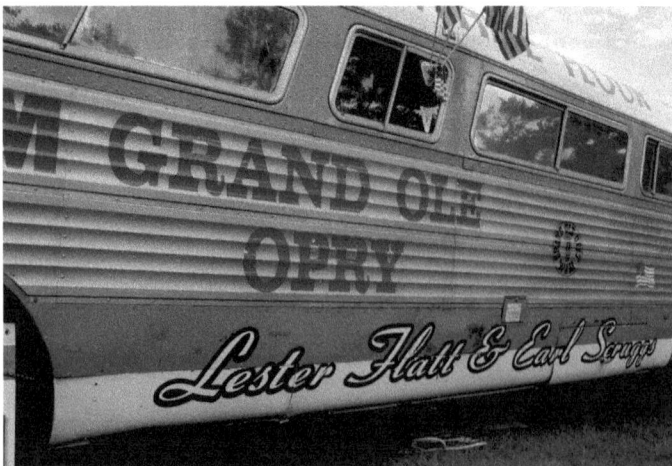

QUESTION 249

Pete Seeger led the estimated 500,000 in attendance, singing John Lennon's "Give Peace A Chance." Which bluegrass figure also performed in Washington DC at the November 15, 1969 Moratorium to End the War in Vietnam?

A. David Grisman

B. Bill Harrell

C. Red Allen

D. Earl Scruggs

E. Arlo Guthrie

F. Alison Krauss

QUESTION 250

This ought to be an easy one. What was the name of the newspaper Jimmy Brown used to sell?

A. *The Daily News*

B. *The Morning Bugle*

C. *Morning Star*

D. *The Bluegrass Herald*

E. *The Mountain Times*

QUESTION 251

Jim Eanes once said if he were a potter, the only thing he would change would be:

    A. his clothes, twice a day

    B. your name

    C. his name and address

    D. he would get air conditioning in his studio

    E. professions

QUESTION 252

Which artist/group was known as "the voice with a heart"?

    A. Mac Wiseman

    B. Jim McReynolds, of Jim and Jesse

    C. Mountain Heart

    D. Harty Taylor, of Karl & Harty

    E. Roger Sprung

QUESTION 253

Can you supply the last line in the refrain of this Jimmie Skinner song? It's been recorded by Wyatt Rice, Dave Evans, Rock County, the Hagar's Mountain Boys, the River Bottom Bluegrass Band, and more.

> He drank whiskey for his liver
> smoked cigarettes for his lungs
> He loved women for his ego

QUESTION 254

For the record, why *was* Bill Monroe going back to old Kentucky, anyway?

QUESTION 255

What is the antidote to narrow-minded people on the narrow-minded streets?

QUESTION 256

Moving to physical afflictions, what colored beverage is most likely to cause cephalic disorder, namely a swelling of the head?

QUESTION 257

From narrow minds to a swollen head, we turn to restraining orders and tears being shed. There's a pretty young woman involved, a little bitty boy, and a puppy. Can you name the song?

QUESTION 258

On a lovesick theme, imagine that Jimmy Martin was coming home. He may have felt his honey was a little prone to extreme acts. What did he counsel her not to do?

QUESTION 259

The color red shows up in bluegrass now and again. Which one of these five doesn't fit?

    A. Red Rector

    B. Red Smiley

    C. Red Allen

    D. Panama Red

    E. Red White and Bluegrass

QUESTION 260

Where'd the music come from? He got his smile from his mama (his brown eyes from her, too), his working hands from his daddy, his gift of gab from Grandpa, his car from Detroit city, his woman from the country, right here in Tennessee. That ought to be enough clues. Where did he get his music from?

QUESTION 261

Can you supply the next line from a certain song? Here's the first one: "There's magic everywhere when that football's in the air"

QUESTION 262

Name the artist who featured a song with this refrain:

Bluegrass, white snow
Memories and an ol' banjo
Get your fiddle out
Have a look at that bow
Bluegrass, white snow

QUESTION 263

What less than reverent holiday season song contains the lines "My plastic is maxed out" and "My checkbook is red and greenbacks are dear"?

QUESTION 264

Confusing theology? Can you name the bluegrass artist who recorded *Songs of Our Fathers: Traditional Jewish Melodies* AND an entire album of Christmas songs?

QUESTION 265

Here's one of the easiest ones: Name the most famous Tex Logan song made popular by Bill Monroe and the Bluegrass Boys.

QUESTION 266

True or false? Did Jimmy Martin and the Sunny Mountain Boys sing "Will we have room for Jesus on this Christmas Day?"

QUESTION 267

Did the band Volume Five name itself after the Bluegrass Album Band's album, *Volume 5: Sweet Sunny South*?

QUESTION 268

Who popularized the song "The Man Who Invented Daylight Savings Time"?

QUESTION 269

Speaking of theme songs, who wrote "Murder on Music Row," the song most notably made famous by Alan Jackson? There's a connection there to standard time, not daylight savings time.

QUESTION 270

Along a similar theme, what band is known for the song "A Far Cry from Lester and Earl"?

QUESTION 271

Separated at birth? Fats Waller and Charlie Waller.

QUESTION 272

What group recorded a song that ended with this line? I hope that they don't make men like my grandpa anymore.

ANSWERS

1. Since the Dobro tends to be the sixth instrument, we would add the number of strings on the fiddle (4), banjo (5), mandolin (8), guitar (6) and bass (4). That's a total of 27.

2. We'll say "true" but false could be correct, too, if you had in mind the one-day festival in 1961 noted below. Going with the definition of a festival as comprising more than one band and more than one day, it's generally agreed that the first bluegrass festival was held about 12 miles north of Roanoke at Cantrell's Horse Farm in Fincastle, Virginia over Labor Day weekend (September 3, 4, & 5) in 1965. The cost of admission was $6.00 for all three days. The first multi-group festival was a one-day event held at Oak Leaf Park in Luray, Virginia, on July 4, 1961. That festival was an all-star event featuring Bill Monroe and the Blue Grass Boys, The Stanley Brothers, The Country Gentlemen, Jim & Jesse, Mac Wiseman, and Bill Clifton.

Festival poster courtesy of Alice Gerrard.

3. Carlton Haney

4. The correct answer is E. The band was comprised of JD Crowe, Tony Rice, Ricky Skaggs, and Bobby Slone.

5. *BU* first published in 1966. It's still going strong.

6. It was E. *Bluegrass Unlimited*, Vol. 1 No. 7, January 1967 had Carter Stanley on the cover. Current managing editor Linda Shaw adds, "Sadly, the inside text was his obituary."

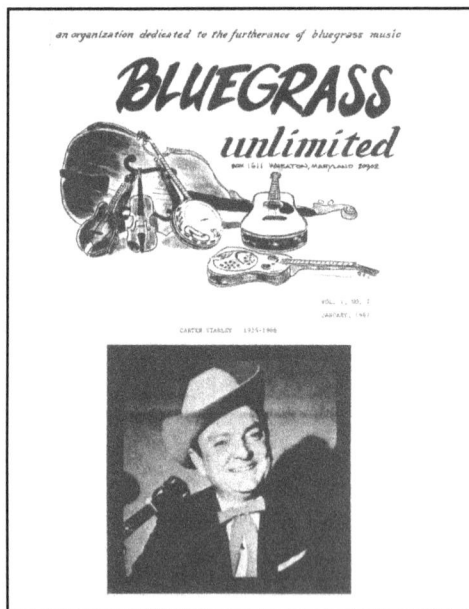

The very first issue, courtesy of Bluegrass Unlimited.

7. B—In March 2011, Dave answered an inquiry, writing, in part, "The main route I worked was New York to Pittsburgh (on the Pennsylvania RR), but I also worked New York to Buffalo (New York Central), New York to Washington, New York to Boston and New York to Springfield (the latter two were on the New Haven trains). I was a substitute who was on call for wherever they needed someone to fill in. In 1964 I had the opportunity to become a 'regular' by moving to Pittsburgh and working the reverse runs (Pittsburgh to NYC). I worked there about a year until I took a leave of absence and started running my business full time (it had started as a hobby about 1962)." Dave added that he really enjoyed the job.

8. D—Bluegrass 45. The band was formed in 1968 by brothers Saburo and Toshio Watanabe. *Run Mountain* was the name of their first album, released in Japan. Akira Otsuka and his brother Tsuyoshi ("Josh") were two other members of the band. Their debut American album, the first of two on Rebel, was eponymous. Saburo, or "Sab", went on to found Japan's B.O.M. Service Co., which for the past 40 years has distributed bluegrass and old-time music in Japan. "Fuji Mountain Breakdown" was recorded by the Bluegrass 45. *Moonshiner* is a publication that Sab started in 1983, to cover the music.

9. Delia Bell. Also known here as "E". The pair recorded three albums for Rounder: *Cheer of the Homefires*, *A Few Dollars More*, and *Following A Feeling*.

10. Ron Thomason, who started Dry Branch Fire Squad in 1976. That was quite a long time ago, wasn't it?

11. It's true. Every one of them.

12. Five. (Did you think it was a trick question?)

13. D — Barry Mitterhoff wasn't one of that band.

14. C — the Vern Williams Band

15. B — Stringbean (Dave Akeman)

16. B — Hazel Dickens. Her song was included on the first *Hazel & Alice* album, released in 1973 as Rounder 0027.

The classic first Rounder album by Hazel & Alice.

17. C — James Pendleton Vandiver was Bill's uncle, known as Uncle Pen.

18. E — Bean Blossom, held in the southern Indiana Brown County community of that name since June 1967.

19. "Blue Moon of Kentucky" was the B side of Sun 209, the first single 45-rpm record recorded by Elvis Presley, and released in 1954. The A side was Arthur "Big Boy" Crudup's song "That's All Right Mama."

20. C—Bessie Lee Mauldin played bass from 1953-1964. Lester Flatt played guitar for almost a full three years. Jimmy Martin had a similar tenure, but a few months less than Lester. Howdy Forrester was in the band twice in the Forties, but only for about four months each time. Kenny Baker served longer than any of the others among our choices, but in three different stints.

21. B—Wilene Forrester, given the nickname "Sally Ann" by Bill. Forrester was known as "Billie" (but no one other than Bill himself could have a nickname like that while in Bill's band) and was married to Howdy Forrester. She played as a Blue Grass Boy from 1943 into early 1946, and recorded on eight tracks in 1945. She was one of the few people who ever sang tenor to Bill Monroe.

22.   C — Jenny Lynn. That was the name of a fiddle tune played by Bill's uncle Pen. From the song Bill wrote:
      He played an old piece he called "Soldier's Joy"
      And the one called "The Boston Boy"
      The greatest of all was "Jenny Lynn"
      To me that's where the fiddle begins.

23.   C — Bluegrass Music. After all, is someone is the Father of Bluegrass Music, then his son must be…Bluegrass Music. Bill did have a son, and named him James William Monroe. He couldn't be the son of bluegrass music; that would make Bill his grandfather.

24.   James William Monroe II, a/k/a Jimbo. As just explained, Bill Monroe's son was named James William Monroe. Therefore, if Bill was the father of Bluegrass Music, James was Bluegrass Music. And James (defined thus as Bluegrass Music) had a son himself, who he named James II. One way or another, Bill Monroe was the grandfather of James William Monroe II.

25.   That would be C — Jimmie Rodgers.

26.   Chief Powhatan — selection B. We admit it, though. We've not researched his genealogy.

27.   It was the banjo. With Bill, Del played guitar from February 1963 to February 1964. Brad Keith was on banjo for the first 10 months of Del's time with the band.

28. E for excellence. John Herald did a wonderful version of the Marty Robbins song on the second Vanguard album by The Greenbriar Boys, *Ragged But Right!*

29. It certainly wouldn't be F—there was never a bluegrass label spelled Adzam Aruha. For that matter, there was never one spelled Ahura Mazda, either. Ahura Mazda is the name given to the supreme deity in the Zoroastrian religion. There was, however, a blues record label with that name, which Rounder Distribution used to help market. Let's look at the others:

Leber spelled backwards is Rebel. But the label's name was never Leber. Vetco was based in Cincinnati, but if you spell its name backwards, it becomes Octev—sounds a bit like octave but that doesn't really get us anywhere. Spell County backwards and you get Ytnuoc—which sounds like a Mexican entity of some kind but probably is just nonsense. If you spell Marietta backwards, you get Atteiram—a bluegrass record label, but the question asked what label spelled its name backwards. Marietta wasn't the label; Atteiram was the label—but Atteiram wasn't one of the choices. That leaves Renovah. Spell it backwards and you get Hanover. That's not an accident. It's where the name came from.

Now, you ask, why would a label based in Liberty NY name itself after another community in Hanover PA—more than 230 miles distant? The reason may have been love. Rumor has it that founder Paul Gerry had a bit of a crush on bluegrass musician and singer Gloria Belle, and she did come from Hanover (and, as of 2011, still has relatives there).

30. Some of these questions are easy, we know. Asked what else in life you could possibly need besides a pig in a pen and corn to feed him on, there can really only be one other thing you need. The correct answer is:

All I need's a pretty little girl
To feed him when I'm gone

Of course, if you happen to be a woman, the answer can be modified slightly if you wish. The same is true for gay men or women, or for confirmed hermits. Heck, you might not really need anything else other than someone who you could hire to come by and feed your pig.

A pigpen in Texas. Photography by Russell Lee, WPA.

31. A—the Osborne Brothers. Now, Alison Krauss has played there—both for the Clintons and the Obamas, but the Osbornes played at the White House on March 17, 1973 for President Richard M. Nixon and family. It was almost a full 17 months later before the President resigned, so there appears not to be any cause and effect. We'd further note that Alison still hadn't reached her second birthday at that time. She started young, but not that young.

32. C—Earl Taylor and the Stony Mountain Boys. In April 1959, Alan Lomax produced the "Folksong '59" concert, which also saw Muddy Waters, Memphis Slim, The Cadillacs, Pete Seeger, and Mike Seeger grace the Carnegie Hall stage.

33. We're on a roll with C. There ain't no smoggy smoke on Rocky Top and there ain't no telephone bills. There was, however, a girl who was half bear, other half cat, wild as a mink, but sweet as soda pop. There wasn't any corn or likely much growth at all—it was rocky, after all! Certainly corn won't grow at all on Rocky Top. Dirt's too rocky by far. There's definitely a chance that an old-time banjo man may have visited at one time or another, but we have no direct knowledge of that.

34. That's a D. There were six albums, and Todd Phillips played bass on 'em all—except #5, which featured Mark Schatz.

35. This one's B. Drusilla's dad founded Blue Ridge Records, and she became very active with the label. Speaking of Drusilla Adams, we'd like to get in touch with her! If anyone out there knows how to reach her (we understand that she became Drusilla Adams Smith through marriage), please ask them to contact Bill Nowlin at Rounder Records. bnowlin@rounder.com is one way. Or call 617-413-8283 and leave a message. Please. You might win a (very) modest reward.

36. E — Frank Wakefield, or — as he is sometimes known — Wake Frankfield. As the number 16 indicates, it wasn't the first tune with a title beginning "Jesus Loves His Mandolin Player."

Rounder 0007.

37. True. Tex Logan and Don Stover were among the other musicians performing at the Mexico City games.

38. Ray Brewster—thus, the correct selection is A. The November 2009 issue of *Bluegrass Unlimited*—which featured the Steep Canyon Rangers on the cover—has a detailed story of the events. It's a pretty shocking story.

39. B—Hot Rize. And if you're tempted to sing the jingle, this could help, from the Flatt & Scruggs version:

Now you bake right (uh-huh) with Martha White (yes, ma'am)
Goodness gracious, good and light, Martha White

For the finest biscuits, cakes and pies,
Get Martha White self-rising flour
The one all purpose flour,
Martha White self-rising flour's
Got Hot Rise

For the finest cornbread you can bake,
Get Martha White self-rising meal

The one all purpose meal
Martha White self-rising meal
For goodness' sake

Disclaimer: this was not a product placement. Martha White Flour unfortunately in no way subsidized this book.

40. A—Barry Poss, founder of Sugar Hill Records. Steve Harris was Rounder's second paid employee, but how many people know that? He did play a little guitar but never recorded for Rounder. Chris Jones is, among other things, a disc jockey on Sirius XM Radio, but was not a Rounder recording artist.

41. C stands for Colwell. The Colwell Brothers who came to California from Detroit via Massachusetts and cut "Bluebonnet Lane" in 1952. They did a lot of radio and TV work, including the *Tex Williams Show*. They went on the road with Moral Rearmament and found themselves on, in effect, an 11-year long world tour, playing bluegrass-rooted music in some 60 countries from 1953 to 1964, then came back to America and in 1965 provided the leadership for the show that became Up with People.

42. C again—Lester and Earl never had a woman in the Foggy Mountain Boys band. Blue Rose, conversely, didn't have a man in their group.

43. C—As the singer said, "Everybody I met seemed to be a rank stranger."

44. B—"White Dove," a song made most famous by the Stanley Brothers.

45. C—"Bringing Mary Home," a song made most famous by the Country Gentlemen

46. Old Ten Brooks was a-flyin'

47. E—Byron Berline, who also played on sessions with The Band, The Byrds, John Denver, Bob Dylan, The Eagles, and…Henry Mancini.

48. D—Dailey & Vincent. NO, JUST KIDDING! It is B—The Sally Mountain Show, the family group with which she first played mandolin at age eight.

49. Jim & Jesse McReynolds played together for a full 55 years, ending with Jim's passing on December 31, 2002. The correct answer is, therefore, E.

50. C stands for Compass. Alison Brown and Garry West founded Compass Records in 1994, and it has become an important source for Celtic, Americana, and bluegrass music. David Grisman did, too, but he wasn't on the list. David founded Acoustic Disc back in 1990. If you guessed Jimmie Skinner, OK, we'll give you credit for that one. Jimmie was a country and bluegrass singer, and it appears that both Skinner and Lou Ukelson were involved with ownership.

51. C again—the Tennessee Cut-Ups

52. B—Clarence was born in Gate City, Virginia in 1931 and died in Jonesborough, Tennessee in 2007. He worked as a fiddler and sideman with, among others, The Sauceman Brothers, The Bailey Brothers, Bill Monroe, Jimmy Martin, Carl Story, Hylo Brown, Jim Eanes, Red Smiley, Lester Flatt, and Patty Loveless.

53. B — the Bay State (Massachusetts). Though natives of West Virginia, with an established career in West Virginia and Tennessee running from 1938 to 1950, the band relocated to the Boston area and for 16 years played seven nights a week at the downtown Hillbilly Ranch with just two weeks vacation as time off.

54. C — Eli Lilly formed a major pharmaceutical company based in Indiana, Eli Lilly & Company. He died in 1898, well before bluegrass music was born.

55. E — Scotty Stoneman, son of Ernest V. "Pop" Stoneman and the rather busy Hattie Frost Stoneman. Only 13 of the children survived into adulthood, but even then it must have been difficult to remember everyone's name, much less their birthdays.

56. D — Bill's older brother Birch played bass and fiddle in the years 1945 through 1947. Charlie had, of course, been Bill's partner in The Monroe Brothers but never played as a member of the Blue Grass Boys. The others were all Monroe brothers, but not part of the band.

57. Al Hawkes — B — founded Event Records.

58.   A, as explained in the song "White House Blues"

McKinley hollered, McKinley squalled
Doctor said, "McKinley I can't find the ball.
You're bound to die, you're bound to die."

The White House, 1907. Courtesy Library of Congress.

59.   B — guitar.

60.   C — though it's safe to say they are less famous than the others, they're the only twins on the list.

61.   C — "The Last Song" was a song, but not an album title. If you want to hear a great new version of the song, check out Josh Williams.

62. Sorry—that was a trick. They've all been subject of one or more tribute albums. Jim & Jesse's 1965 album *Berry Pickin' in the Country* for Epic was the first, a year before the Charles River Valley Boys released *Beatle Country*.

63. Pretty improbable, right? But it's true.

64. We don't know the answer, since it's *your* mind we're talking about. But for most people, it would be C—Lester Flatt, even though the song was actually sung by Jerry Scroggins, while Lester and Earl played the music.

65. A—Bill Monroe, who ran a team called the Bluegrass All-Stars. Don Reno recalled when he'd taken over Earl Scruggs' place in the band, "Bill was more interested in ball than he was in music at this time. I reckon this was a way of resting his mind from music. But he liked to kill me playing ball. We would work a show one night and drive to the next town and usually get in at an early morning hour, and he'd have a ball game set up by ten o'clock with the local team." (From *Bossmen: Bill Monroe & Muddy Waters* by Jim Rooney)

66. Pat Enright, though he was a member of Tasty Licks, Dreadful Snakes, the Nashville Bluegrass Band, and one of the voices of the Soggy Bottom Boys. Neither was Kimber Ludiker.

67. False. That was how Ralph Stanley used to describe Jack Cooke.

68. B—Larry Rice, who was a member of J. D. Crowe and the Kentucky Mountain Boys in the late 1960s.

69. B—When he joined the Stanley Brothers, Ralph Meadows became Joe.

70. C—The answer is Dee.

71. E—It was Larry Sparks.

72. E again, unless "murder by snake" counts. Murder is normally considered to be the willful killing of one human being by another human being.

73. E yet again—John Pennell

74. C—Bill Emerson was a founding member of Country Current, a bluegrass group within the U. S. Navy band.

75. It's back to E. Ralph Stanley was age 72 when he became a member of the Opry in the year 2000.

76. D—Dolly Parton

77. E—Arnold Birch

78. A—Jerry Douglas

79. Jimmy Martin and the Sunny Mountain Boys—E again.

80. True. And the song was reportedly so popular it helped bring King Records back from the brink of bankruptcy.

81. Pete Wernick—E

82. A—Jim Mills, with six

83. Stuart Duncan and Michael Cleveland are both tied, with eight apiece.

84. C—Rob Ickes

85. D—Ronnie McCoury

86. E—Tex Logan

87. True. This William S. Monroe was an infielder who played for 19 years, from 1896 to 1914.

88. E—None of the above. It was a song, not an actual person.

89. They were actually Red Knuckles and the Trailblazers flyswatters, but Red and his group always traveled with Hot Rize and shared the same merch table. E.

90. B—Ola Belle Reed

91. False, in that Grisman's father was a trombonist. He was a professional player, though, and David's first recording was in 1963 for Folkways with Red Allen, Frank Wakefield, and the Kentuckians.

92. B—It was March 5, 1960 that the Osborne Brothers played at An-
     tioch College in Yellow Springs, Ohio.

93. That's true. And they are musical brothers from different mothers.

94. E—Jimmy Brown

95. E—Dan Tyminski

Dan Tyminski. Courtesy of Rounder Records.

96. That's completely untrue.

97. D—Joe repaired typewriters

98. B—Bill Monroe's *Southern Flavor* won the Grammy Award in 1989, the first year a Grammy was granted in the newly-established Grammy field.

99. The answer is A *and* D, but the one who was a bluegrass musician is Eddie Adcock.

100. C—Clarence White was killed by a drunken driver on July 15, 1973.

101. True. In 1955, J.D. spent the summer with Mac Wiseman, and then went on to play with Jimmy from 1956 into 1961, but he had also played part of the summer of 1954 with Jimmy Martin.

102. E's the correct response. And it did sound good.

103. C—the Foundation. Or so we were led to believe.

104. D—Rich-R-Tone. In the 1970s, Rounder released *The Rich-R-Tone Story,* presenting a selection of recordings from Stanton's label along with a booklet detailing the story. It was Rounder 1017, part of Early Days of Bluegrass series.

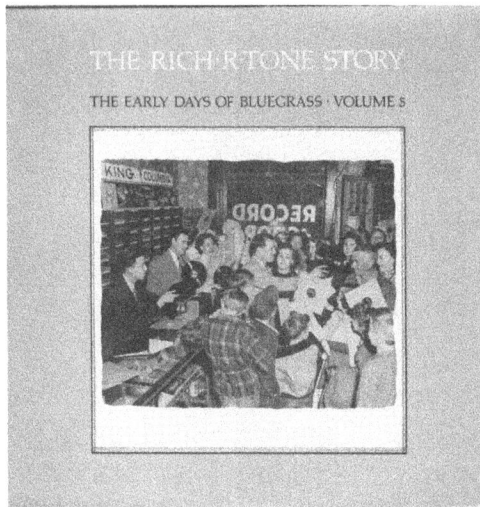

Original LP cover.

105. D.

106. False. Skaggs had already turned 15.

107. A Whole Lot More of Jesus (And A Lot Less Rock & Roll)—according to the Wayne Raney song by that title. The Greenbriar Boys repopularized the song, for new audiences.

108. All of them!

109. E—The 1995 album *Now That I Found You* by Alison Krauss and Union Station was the first. The Nitty Gritty Dirt Band album *Will The Circle Be Unbroken* went platinum, too...but, hey, they're not a bluegrass group.

110. A—Wayne Lewis, from May 1976 to May 1986.

111. False.

112. B—Dry Branch Fire Squad.

113. Vassar Clements.

114. C—Alison Krauss joined the Opry in 1993, when she was 21. At the time, she was the first bluegrass artist (of any age) who had joined the Opry in 29 years. But Carol Lee Cooper was just 14 when she joined the Opry along with her parents, Wilma Lee and Stoney Cooper, in 1957.

115. Until paroled, he served 31 years of a 40-year prison sentence at La-Grange Correctional Institute in Kentucky. His real name was Harry Shelor, though he wasn't sentenced for playing in a bluegrass band under a false name. He was sentenced for killing a man. He'd perhaps taken too many murder ballads to heart. He was released in 2013.

116. False. The other is Vaughn Monroe. Woody Woodpecker's got a star, as does Rin Tin Tin and E. Power Biggs.

117. The answer is C and D (John Hartford and Steve Martin).

118. The answer is both D and E. Sierra was 15 when she first recorded for Rounder. George Pegram was in his 70s.

119. True. And he got all the way to Bean Blossom, but Richard D. Smith in his Monroe biography *Can't You Hear Me Callin'* writes, "Intimidated by the mere sight of the formidable Kentuckian, Garcia went back home without even speaking to Bill."

120. We thought that Fred Bartenstein was the first, and only, editor. He corrects us by writing, "The late Kathy Kaplan, New York City-based radio personality and bluegrass scholar, edited the first issue, Volume 1, Number 1, dated August, 1969, for publisher Carlton Haney.... Months went by and nothing further was heard from *Muleskinner News*. I felt bad about this and took it upon myself to produce Volume 1, Number 2, dated February, 1970. I served as editor and recruited a staff of contributing editors, including Kathy Kaplan, Bill Vernon, Peggy (Mrs. Tex) Logan, and "Ranger" Doug Green....My last issue was Volume 6, Number 1, dated January, 1975."

121. True. Bill Hurst was apparently very well-connected in his part of Kentucky. Ralph Stanley's autobiography, *Man of Constant Sorrow: My Life and Times*, details more of the story.

122. D — Roland LeBlanc a/k/a Roland White

123. If you said Bob Paisley and Danny Paisley, you'd be right. You could also have named Del McCoury, and Ronnie & Rob McCoury.

124. Tony Trischka, who was on the first Country Cooking album.
      F.   Use Trischka here

125. It was David Grisman who did.

126. Yup—Scott Billington, on harmonica.

127. B—Charles Sizemore, Esq., who is licensed to practice in Kentucky and Tennessee, a member of both the Tennessee and Kentucky Bar Associations. Blaine Sprouse would have been a good guess, too, but he wasn't on the list. And neither was David Crow, but he would have been an excellent choice as well. Ditto Johnny Lewis.

128. The follow-up album was *O Sister*, a collection of songs by women in bluegrass released on Rounder Records.

O SISTER!
THE WOMEN'S BLUEGRASS COLLECTION

129. The band is The Grascals. More importantly, the banjo player is Kristin Scott Benson. Her grandfather was Arval Hogan, and she named her son Hogan after her grandfather.

130. B—Ralph Stanley. Stratton was the post office at the time. It is, Ralph says, "a very small place right close to McClure." (See John Wright's book *Traveling the High Way Home*, p. 44.)

131. A—Wade Mainer was born on April 21, 1907 and grew up in a log cabin near Weaverville, North Carolina. As of opening day of the 2011 baseball season, he was still alive, closing in on his 104th birthday. He passed away in 2012. Mac Wiseman turned 90 in the year 2015; that's pretty impressive, too.

132. We should hope so! It's Blue Highway, which played its first show on New Year's Eve 1994. Earlier bands included Dusty Miller and Alison Krauss & Union Station. A song he co-wrote, "Through the Window of a Train," was the IBMA Song of the Year in 2008.

133. There was a huge hint among the answers to question #130: they are all members of the Cox Family. And if you drive into Cotton Valley, Louisiana you will see a sign informing you that it is "Home of the Cox Family." Late in 2015, they released their first album in many years: *Gone Like the Cotton*.

134. There is a Charles River, which separates Boston and Cambridge, Massachusetts near its mouth, not far from the green playing fields of Harvard University. It's 80 miles long, with all its twists and turns, and has its source in Hopkinton, from where the Boston Marathon begins (it's just a short 26.2 mile run to the finish line, on a route which clearly doesn't follow the river). We wouldn't normally quote from Wikipedia, but their explanation of the origin of the name is succinct: "Captain John Smith explored and mapped the coast of New England, naming many features including the Charles River, which he gave the Native American name, Massachusetts River. When Smith presented his map to [England's King] Charles I he suggested that the king should feel free to change any of the 'barbarous names' for 'English' ones." With the modesty befitting a king of the time, he named the River Charles for himself.

135. The Dobro. The name also appealed to John Dopyera and his brother Ed (born Emil) when they formed the Dobro Manufacturing Company in 1928. It's a contraction of "Dopyera" and "brothers" and they also liked it because the word itself meant "good" in their native tongue. One of the early slogans of the company was "Dobro means good in any language."

136. Lloyd Loar, most known in bluegrass circles for his F-5 mandolins created for Gibson.

137. A—*High Lonesome*, a 1991 production.

138. Daley & Vincent.

139. Jerry Douglas, whose first two album titles drew on his nickname: *Fluxology* and *Fluxedo*.

140. Alison Krauss. The 1987 album was *Too Late to Cry* and it was dedicated to the Columbia Middle School of Champaign, Illinois. She was 15 years old when the album was recorded.

141. The Kentucky Colonels.

142. The author was Don Stover.

143. Hazel Dickens.

144. Andy Statman. The track is featured on his album *Nashville Mornings New York Nights* (Rounder 0174).

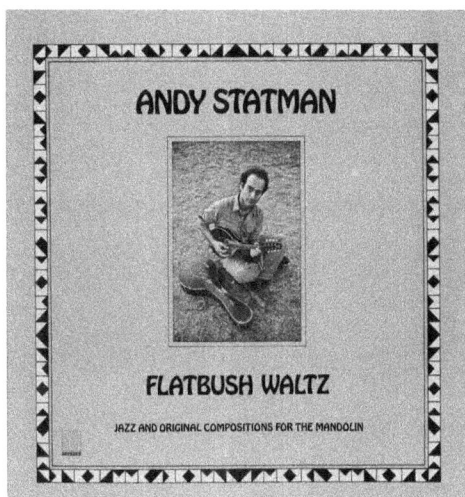

ANDY STATMAN

FLATBUSH WALTZ

JAZZ AND ORIGINAL COMPOSITIONS FOR THE MANDOLIN

145. True. He did.

146. Walter Browning's golden wedding ring.

147. "Home Run Man"—first made famous by Jimmy Martin.

148. Yes, Carter Stanley was a Blue Grass Boy from July 1951 until October 1951. Though only for a couple of pickup dates, Ralph also played very briefly.

149. You could have just answered "yes" or "no"—but in case you were wondering what the correct answer is: Yes, it was Billy Pack.

150. Terry Eldridge. The song is also sung by the Cleverly Trio and a version can be found on YouTube.

151. None. But Ralph won the 2001 Grammy for Best Male Country Vocal Performance with his version of "O Death."

152. Country Cooking. The printers didn't know it was the name of a musical group and gave it huge, prominent billing on the posters.

153. Bringin' my baby back.

154. Vassar Clements, who was born in 1928, making him 14 years older (and grayer) than 1942 babies Peter Rowan (July 4) and Jerry Garcia (August 1).

155. It is true.

156. There is probably more than one. We were thinking of King Wilkie, named after Bill Monroe's horse. It's a band which plays much more than bluegrass, however, so perhaps it's not—strictly speaking—a bluegrass band.

157. Smilin' Jim Eanes, who cut Arthur Smith's song "I Took Her by Her Little Brown Hand" for Rich-R'-Tone. As Pete Kuykendall has written, "It told quite a unique story of an interracial romance and, for its day and time—the early 50s, was not the exact record to be expected from a traditional country performer. Jim featured the number on all his appearances and there was little if any adverse reaction to its message." When Jim signed to Decca, however, they asked him to drop both the banjo and the direct reference to race. Eanes told Kuykendall, "I never had anybody question me at all about the song until I cut it for Decca." [*Bluegrass Unlimited*, February 1973]

158. Larry Sparks—because of his song "John Deere Tractor."

159. Ralph Rinzler of the Greenbriar Boys, who founded the Festival of American Folklife and served the director of its office of folk-life programs. He worked as the Smithsonian's assistant secretary for public service from 1983 to 1990.

160. Rhonda Vincent.

161. Ralph Rinzler, the same guy who was the answer to #159.

162. Yes, he did it. He slipped poison into her little glass of wine, but poisoned himself as well. They folded their arms around each other and they cast their eyes unto the sky. We know this, because the Stanley Brothers told us about it in their Rich-R-Tone recording, "Little Glass of Wine."

163. Lazarus and Jesus. In the case of Lazarus's sad fate, he lay down at the rich man's gate and begged for the crumbs from the rich man to eat. He was some mother's darlin', he was some mother's son. Once he was fair and once he was young. Some mother rocked him, her darlin' to sleep. But they left him to die like a tramp on the street.

164. Robert C. Byrd, who presented a copy of his 1978 album *Mountain Fiddler* to Russian President Leonid Brezhnev. Byrd was raised by his uncle and aunt, Titus and Vlurma Byrd.

165. The SteelDrivers.

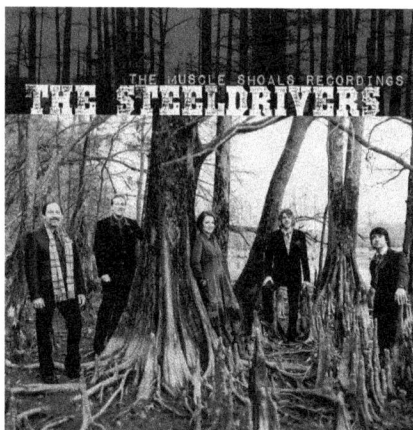

This 2015 release by the SteelDrivers was a Grammy finalist.

166. According to answers.com, here's the story: Work with the Blue Grass Boys was very challenging for Flatt in particular. As Neil Rosenberg explains, the tempo Monroe set in much of his music was daunting, and Flatt had to improvise to keep up. "Monroe was playing much of his music so fast that Lester had trouble keeping time on the guitar," writes Rosenberg. "He solved this problem by catching up at the ends of phrases with a guitar run which, in its fullest form in the key of G, slid from F-sharp to G on the sixth string, then from A to B on the fifth string, from D to E on the fourth and ended in a ringing open G note on the third string. Often only the end of the run was audible. This was a common phrase in country guitar playing long before Lester used it, but because he used it so frequently and effectively it became associated with him, and eventually with bluegrass music, as 'the Lester Flatt G run'."

167. The answer follows a little explanation. The WWNC and WOPI slogans are both accurate. The slogan for WPTF is correct, too; the station was owned by the Durham Life Insurance Company. Likewise, WSM was owned by an insurance company, the National Life and Accident Insurance Company, and "We Shield Millions" was indeed their slogan. Radio station WCYB was owned by the Tri-Cities Assurance Company and its original slogan was "We Cover Your Butt"—but it was deemed too saucy and quickly replaced. Actually, that's not true at all. Neither the name of the assurance company nor either slogan indicated was associated with the station. We don't really know whether there ever was an associated slogan. The answer is C.

168. That would be Jesse McReynolds.

169. Mac Wiseman.

170. The 1972 film *Deliverance*, which took up a tune called "Feudin' Banjos" by Arthur "Guitar Boogie" Smith and made it popular—too popular, according to some who were driven to distraction.

171. Eric Weissberg and Steve Mandell.

172. Claire Lynch, currently of the Claire Lynch Band.

Claire Lynch, courtesy of Rounder Records.

173. Of the groups listed, the most venerable among them was Reno & Smiley and the Tennessee Cut-Ups, after Red's death known as Don Reno, Bill Harrell & the Tennessee Cut-Ups.

174. Chances are there is more than one, but the one we are thinking of is Hubert Davis who owned The Bluegrass Inn, in Nashville.

175. Sierra Hull.

176. That good old mountain dew.

177. Doc had never recorded for Rounder at the time, nor written any songs released on Rounder, so — as was also the case with President Gerald R. Ford — Rounder didn't owe him any royalties.

178. It's Carl Jackson.

179. Birth name: William Marburg. Name in bluegrass: Bill Clifton.

180. Mike Seeger.

181. God.

   Oh you don't love God, if you don't love your neighbor
   if you gossip about him, if you never have mercy
   if he gets into trouble, and you don't try to help him
   then you don't love your neighbor, and you don't love God

182. Go stepping, too! After all, the bait ain't what it used to be and I've
   got news for you:

   I'll go stepping too, my honey
   I'll go stepping too
   I'll lock the door, put out the cat
   And I'll go stepping too

183. I'll keep on loving you.

184. For that Blue Ridge far away. When you get there, you'll see your
   old dog Trey and two heads of snowy white.

185. He will set your fields on fire!

186. My old paint horse.

187. I found I had a cinder all covered up in white. That old sugar coated love is something I can't bite.

188. Fly over the prison walls, and fly to the arms of your darling—where you would be willing to die.

189. Love em and leave em, kiss em and grieve em; that used to be my motto so high…I used to be a killer with the women me oh my. But now I'm just a hot shot with a teardrop in my eye.

190. Your home is on your back. You know every inch of highway and every foot of back road, every mile of railroad track.

191. A little place called Hamburger Dan's.

192. D—he was 14, and the youngest to record with the band.

193. Roland.

194. Arnold Shultz.

195. Scotty Stoneman.

196. There might, arguably, be others, but were you able to find 10 from the list which follows? Billy Baker, Kenny Baker, Bill Box, Gene Christian, Porter Church (both his first and last names qualify, as do Bill Box's), Jack Cooke, Dana Cupp, Howdy Forrester, Joe Forrester, Bob Fowler, Ernest Graves, Lonnie Hoppers, Joe Meadows, Skip Payne, Dale Potter, Bill Price, Pete Pyle, Butch Robins, Billy Rose, Bobby Smith, Charlie Smith, Roger Smith, Mark Squires, Art Stamper, Carl Story, Chick Stripling, Red Taylor, Howard Watts.

197. Examples include: The Whites, Richard Greene, Bob Black, Red Allen, Bud Rose, Tom Gray, Alison Brown. No, Tan Dyminski does not quality. If Charles J. Tan expands his repertoire, he might qualify. Of course, the same goes for Pink. There is a band called the Purple Hulls. Of course, we do have Blue Highway, too, if you want to get into group names. There's a French band named Turquoise. We also have Amber Collins, and the fairly-unknown Joshua Lavender, and we're sure there are others. And, speaking of Hulls, Benjamin Moore has a number of paint colors with the word "Sierra" as part of them, such as Sierra Hills 1053.

198. In the November/December 1987 interview, Bob Dylan said, "The stuff that I grew up on never grows old. I was just fortunate enough to get it and understand it at that early age, and it still rings true for me. I'd still rather listen to Bill and Charlie Monroe than any current record. That's what America's all about to me. I mean, they don't have to make any more new records -- there's enough old ones, you know?"

199. True — but that would be Charlie Monroe's band, the Kentucky Pardners, in 1943.

200. Ralph Stanley was awarded an honorary degree by Lincoln Memorial University of Harrogate, Tennessee in 1976. Dr. Stanley was also awarded the National Medal of Arts in 2006.

201. This is not objective fact, but since this bluegrass trivia book is being put together as the Rounder Book, we admit to a certain bias and subjectivity. It's just a matter of opinion, of course, but we think the answer is: All of the above, except E. Perceptive readers will notice quite a few references to Rounder throughout this, perhaps reflecting its genesis. We're nothing if not a little passionate about the music and the musicians with whom we've been able to work.

202. That's a pretty heavy question. The answer rests within you.

203. True. As Bill Malone writes in *Stars of Country Music*, Joplin was a performer at Threadgill's in Austin and "In those pre-rock and pre-San Francisco days, Joplin performed with a bluegrass group called the Waller Creek Boys, strummed an autoharp, and sang Carter Family songs and gospel tunes in addition to the country blues which were then dearest to her heart." (See pages 437-8.)

204. D—He spoke not a word though it meant his life, for he had been in the arms of his best friend's wife.

205. It was A—the Earls of Leicester, performing the music of Flatt and Scruggs. They received a Grammy nomination—and won.

206. Alison Brown founded Compass Records, with Garry West, in 1994.

207. Béla Anton Leoš Fleck is named after Hungarian composer Béla Bartók, Austrian composer Anton Webern, and Czech composer Leoš Janáček.

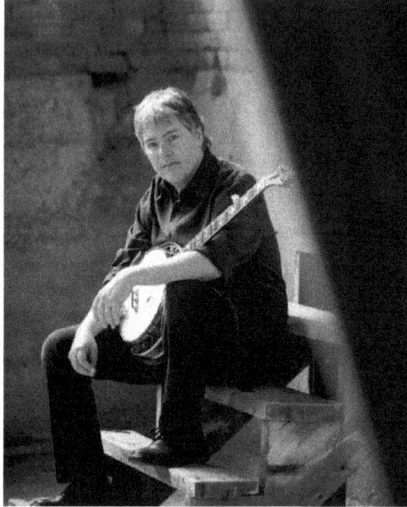

Bela Fleck, courtesy of Rounder Records.

208. Time flies. Yes, the band formed in the year 1971. At least, that's what it says on Wikipedia, so it must be true. Or maybe 1972, when they released their first record, on Starday.

209. Carl Story (who was, incidentally, *not* known for singing story songs).

210. John Paul Jones of Led Zeppelin produced the Uncle Earl's album *Waterloo, Tennessee.*

211. The two guys named Earl. They were guys. No one in Uncle Earl was a guy.

212. Bill Monroe.

213. They all have the same last name. Little Roy and Polly were brother and sister, but Laurie was no known relation. Her father was a classical flute player, but he did once give her an album by Chubby Wise and the Rainbow Ranch Boys.

214. Abigail Washburn and Bela Fleck named their first-born Juno, the name given to the Canadian equivalent of the Grammy Award.

215. Each one of them has the name of a college or university in it. Smith College, Vassar College, Allen College, Hunter College, Jackson State University, Rice University, and Baker College.

216. Every one of the groups won twice or more, though not necessarily in consecutive order. Only Dailey and Vincent and Del McCoury won three in a row. Dailey and Vincent won in 2007 through 2009. But Del tops the list, having won five years in a row (1996, 1997, 1998, 1999, 2000) and then, after a year off, came back and won three times in a row again (2002, 2003, 2004).

217. There really is a Johnson Mountain (more than one, actually), but there's one in Washington State's North Cascades that's, in some respects, not all that far from Steep Canyon, near Diamond Bar, California.

218. They weren't guys at all. The names are the maiden names of Mrs. Scruggs and Mrs. Flatt: Louise Certain and Gladys Stacey. As it happens, they may not have written all the songs attributed to them. Rumor has it that Lester and Earl wrote some of them, as did other members of the group.

219. You might actually do any of those things, but the answer from a bluegrass perspective is A, and you might just find that just a little talk with Jesus makes it right.

220. It was B. Don't you remember? We already covered that in question #135.

221. Mother's not dead, she's only a-sleeping. Just patiently waiting for Jesus to come. The correct answer is C (though admittedly there might well other songs that suggest the other alternatives—but we submit those aren't as famous.)

222. The answer is D. Sophronie left him so lonely. It seems he really cared for her, but she's found another man. And now he has teardrops in his eyes.

223. If you favor shady dealing, then you better do some kneeling! "Big Rock in the Road"—Clyde Moody

224. Scotland, and Jerusalem (the latter separate from his mention of "Jerusalem Ridge," which is a geographic place in Kentucky.

225. Boston, Cheyenne, and Tallahassee.

226. The answer is, unsurprisingly for the man who is credited with creating bluegrass: Kentucky, which is mentioned in at least 11 of those 25 song titles. Told you it wasn't necessarily a trick question.

227. It was a tie: Georgia and Texas, with three each. Ohio and Tennessee each had two song title mentions.

228. "He Will Set Your Soul on Fire."

229. The song is Charlie Sizemore's "Alison's Band," in which he mentions Alison Krauss, Dan Tyminski, Jerry Douglas, Ron Block, and Barry Bales—all of whom constitute Alison Krauss and Union Station.

230. "In Despair" by Joe Ahr and Juanita Pennington.

231. The singer says, "I'm not living. I only exist."

232. Daniel did.

233. "Home Run Man" by Jimmy Martin. See also the related question at #147.

234. "Christmas Time's A Comin'" which was recorded by Bill Monroe.

235. Red was born as Arthur Lee Smiley, in Asheville in 1925. Don Reno was Don Wesley Reno and born in Buffalo, South Carolina in 1927.

236. It's an entirely different song, and they certainly weren't looking for another baby down the line when they sang it, but while searching for more meaning in life they sang another song, a Mac Wiseman song they also recorded for King that year, "I'm Using My Bible for a Roadmap." The last stop was Heaven some sweet day.

237. A. The answer is most likely C. One might think the answer was that they were washed in the blood of the lamb, however counterintuitive that may seem. But the song actually talked about the soul-cleansing power of the blood of the lamb, not the clothes-cleansing properties of said blood. It's a rare person among us who would be fully pure of heart and mind. Your garments themselves may be stained with sin, but the song prescribes that you lay them aside and be washed in the blood of the Lamb.

238. Get a dog. It's a Billy Currington song, popularized in bluegrass by Darren Nicholson: "(I Want You To Love Me) Like My Dog (Does)."

239. You had two chances to win. Either A, Dale Ann Bradley, who sings the song "Meanest Lady Cop in East Kentucky," or E, the lady cop in the song.

240. It was a musician. In fact, it was the "father of Blue Grass music"—Bill Monroe. See *Country Music: The Encyclopedia* by Irwin Stambler and Grelun Landon, p. 316, among other sources.

241. Rounder 0044, by J D Crowe and the New South. Some people call it "0044" and some call it "Rounder 0044." Some call it "the Old Home Place album," because that was the first song on side one. But to any true bluegrass aficionado who has a good record collection, or almost any veteran bluegrass musician, and just say "0044"—chances are very good that they'll know exactly what you mean. In fact, when *Bluegrass Unlimited* ran a story celebrating the album's 40th anniversary, the headline on the front cover of the magazine was: "Rounder 0044." (See the issue of September 2015.)

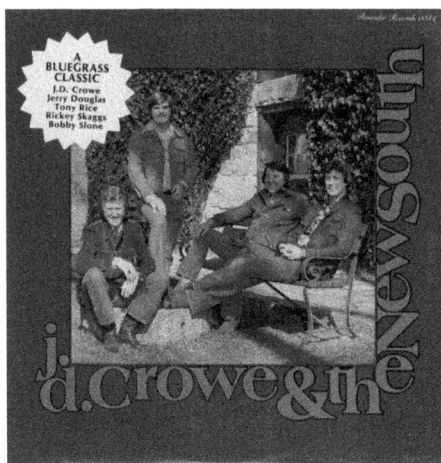

This is the second cover used for 0044. The first one was self-censored after a period of time—but reissued as an LP by Rounder in 2016!

242. Howard Watts. He didn't change his actual name, but with Bill Monroe and the Blue Grass Boys he was typically known by the stage name Cedric Rainwater. With Flatt & Scruggs, he recorded in 1948 and 1949 as…Howard Watts. By the time of the 1950 session, through 1952, there was another Rainwater on their recordings sessions: Jody Rainwater.

243. That would be the song "Della Mae," written by Tommy Sutton and recorded by Red Allen and the Osborne Brothers.

244. Porter Wagoner recorded it, Wanda Jackson recorded it, Gene Stuart recorded it, but the bluegrass group who did was the group Lost & Found. For good measure, they also advise us that a leopard will never change its spots, a tiger will never change its stripes, you can't change daylight to dark, and a hound dog will never change its bark. The song was written by Ray Pennington.

245. The correct answer is: B—Wanda Anne.

246. The Spinney Brothers, from the Annapolis Valley of Nova Scotia. The song, "I'm So Proud To Be Your Dad," is a very moving one of special interest to anyone associated with adoption, written by Rick Spinney. The last two lines of the chorus: "You're the best son that I never had. Although I'm not your father, I'm so proud to be your dad."

247. How could someone make up a story like that? Yes, bizarrely, it's true. But the trick is that the Dillards who fired him weren't the Dillards you were likely thinking of. The timing was about right; it was in 1963 that the bluegrass band known as The Dillards released their first album, *Back Porch Bluegrass*, on the Elektra label. And according to bluegrass scholar Richard Thompson, not too long after 1962, when Gary started his first job, at Radio WFMD in Frederick, Maryland, he took a position with WDON-AM/WASH-FM, owned by the Everett Dillard family. It was a country music station, but Gary played more bluegrass than ownership wanted. Sayonara!

248. Actually, it's a good question. It might have been either *Bonnie & Clyde* or *Deliverance* since the others played bluegrass on a somewhat regular basis, whereas in the two films, the music—although important to the particular scene in which it was prominent—was more limited.

249. A—It was Earl Scruggs with the Earl Scruggs Revue. Alison wasn't even born yet. Did you really think Arlo Guthrie was a bluegrass musician?

250. Let's let the lyrics speak for themselves:

I sell the morning paper, sir,
My name is Jimmy Brown,
Everybody knows I am
The newsboy of the town.

You will hear me yelling "Morning Star,"
As I run along the street.
I have no hat up—on my head,
No shoes upon my feet.

251. In his song "I Wouldn't Change You If I Could," he sang:

And if I were a potter and you a piece of clay
The only thing I'd change would be your name

252. 252. You could have stopped once you hit "A"—it was Mac Wiseman,
and his song "Love Letters in the Sand" exemplified his treatment of
a song (once also recorded by Pat Boone.)

253. "He Died A Rounder at 21." The full refrain:

He drank whiskey for his liver
smoked cigarettes for his lungs
He loved women for his ego
he died a rounder at twenty-one

254. To see his Linda Lou

255. A good antidote might be to shine your light for everyone to see. If you try a little kindness, then you'll overlook the blindness. This is a remedy that's been dispensed by The Osborne Brothers, by Glen Campbell, and a number of others.

256. "If your liquor's too red, it will swell up your head"—that's from the Stanley Brothers' version of "Good Ol' Mountain Dew." The recommended drink—which few refuse—can prove salutary for some, old Uncle Snort, for instance. He was sawed-off and short and measured just 4-foot-2, but he feels like a giant when you give him a pint of that good old mountain dew.

257. Why, the song is "See The Big Man Cry, Mama"—as sung by, among others, Charlie Louvin and Volume Five.

258. In "Hold Whatcha Got," Jimmy urged her, "Don't sell the house, and don't wreck the car." He added, "I'm a comin' home, baby. Stay there, honey, right where you are."

259. Needless to say, it depends on your criteria. One could say that Red White and Bluegrass does not fit, because it's the name of a group and not the name of an individual. Or could say that Panama Red does not fit, because it could be a fictional character or, for that matter, an illegal substance.

260. "When it comes to my music, I got all that from Bill." -- The Spinney Brothers. P.S. If you don't know who Bill is, then, well....

261. "And it's Christmas time on Rocky Top" (as sung by the Osborne Brothers)

262. The artist is Patty Loveless. She titled her album *Bluegrass & White Snow, A Mountain Christmas.*

263. "Bah Humbug" by Tim O'Brien. Which ends, "Chug-a-lug one more eggnog; it's just six more days toil the end of the year."

264. David Grisman cut the first-named album with Andy Statman, and he cut *David Grisman's Acoustic Christmas* for Rounder way back in 1983.

265. None other than "Christmas Time's A-Coming."

266. Yup, he did. In fact, Jimmy released a whole Christmas album on Gusto, entitled *To Mother on Christmas.*

267. Nope. Band leader Glen Harrell explained in a November 29, 2015 e-mail: "When I put this band together I was just trying to come up with something that wasn't so forgettable. I watched a commercial on TV one night and it showed an old stereo with five knobs on it. So I thought about five guys playing music and the listeners liking us and wanting to turn up the volume on the radio of the five guys playing."

268. Grandpa Jones, a/k/a Louis Marshall Jones.

269. That would be Larry Cordle (and Larry Shell), of the group Larry Cordle and Lonesome Standard Time.

270. Junior Sisk and Rambler's Choice.

271. You've got to be kidding. There's no connection at all—or at least none we know of.

272. The Grascals. The song: "Remembering." The reason being that grandpa had a heart of gold hardened into stone by the experiences he suffered in the Second World War.

www.ingramcontent.com/pod-product-compliance
Lightning Source LLC
Chambersburg PA
CBHW072004040426
42447CB00009B/1480